I0560246

# also by colleen m. story

For more information, please see:
colleenmstory.com
masterwritermindset.com

© 2025 by Colleen M. Story. All rights reserved.

No part of this book may be reproduced in any form or by any electronic or mechanical means, including information storage and retrieval systems, without written permission in writing from the publisher or author except by a reviewer, who may quote brief passages in a review.

Although every precaution has been taken to verify the accuracy of the information contained herein, the author and publisher assume no responsibility for any errors or omissions. Further, the publisher does not have any control over and does not assume any responsibility for third-party websites or their content.

No liability is assumed for damages that may result from the use of information contained within. The author does not dispense medical advice or prescribe the use of any technique as a form of treatment for physical, emotional, or medical problems without the advice of a physician, either directly or indirectly. The intent of the author is only to offer information of a general nature to help you in your quest for creative well-being. In the event you use any of the information in this book for yourself, the author and the publisher assume no responsibility for your actions.

Books may be ordered through booksellers or by contacting the publisher at:

Midchannel Press
P.O. Box 131
Iona, ID 83427
www.midchannelpress.com
Email: publisher@midchannelpress.com

To receive a free weekly email newsletter delivering the tools to break through self-doubt, procrastination, and fear so you can write consistently, publish confidently, and build a thriving creative career, register directly at www.masterwritermindset.com/newsletter.

Cover Design: Miblart

ISBN 13: 979-8-9926172-5-2 (Paperback edition)

Library-of-Congress Control Number: 2025909270

First Edition: August 2025, printed in the U.S.A.

# ESCAPE THE WRITER'S WEB

## WORKBOOK

### Action Steps and Exercises to Overcome All 13 Writer Procrastination Types

## COLLEEN M. STORY

# contents

# getting started

# start your escape

**Welcome. I'm so glad you're here.**

I created this workbook as a companion to *Escape the Writer's Web* because I know how hard it can be, as a writer, not just to learn something new but to then turn around and apply it to your creative life.

So often, we read a book that resonates—we underline pages, nod along, feel seen—and then we set it down. Life rushes back in. The web tightens again.

I don't want that to happen to you.

I wrote *Escape the Writer's Web* to help writers understand what procrastination really is: not laziness or poor time management, but a tangled system of emotional patterns that quietly sabotage your progress.

Procrastination hides in fear, perfectionism, self-doubt, overcommitment, disorganization, and distraction.

As the years pass, it doesn't just steal our time, but our confidence, consistency, and, eventually, our belief that we can become the writers we dreamed of being.

That's why I decided to add this workbook as a companion to the main book.

Because I didn't want to stop at insight. I wanted to give you something you could use—a space to explore what's really going on for you and where you can try out practical tools that may help you break free.

In my 25+ years of working with writers, I've seen how determined and passionate so many of us are.

We want to tell stories. We want to write that novel, build that blog, and finish that memoir. But often, we feel stuck because we don't know how to move forward through the invisible barriers we carry.

That's what this workbook is for. To give you a way through.

## HAVE YOU READ "ESCAPE THE WRITER'S WEB?"

Whether you've just finished *Escape the Writer's Web* or you're starting here with the workbook, you're in the right place.

If you have read the book, then you already know your procrastination isn't random or some moral failing. It's part of a deeper emotional pattern that's been subtly (or not so subtly) blocking your writing momentum.

This workbook is your space to take what you've learned and finally apply it in real, creative, personalized ways. You'll go deeper into your type(s), explore tools made for the way you think and work, and start working toward your writing goals, hopefully with more motivation and excitement than you've experienced before.

If you haven't read the book yet, don't worry—you can still start here.

You'll find everything you need to begin. In the next section, you can take the procrastination-type quiz. From there, you'll explore the chapters that match your results. Each one is designed to help you recognize your patterns, shift your mindset, and take small, doable steps forward.

And if you're wondering whether you need to have read the main book to succeed with this workbook: the answer is no, it's not required. But if you're craving deeper insight into why you procrastinate the way you do, *Escape the Writer's Web* is a rich companion to this experience.

It explains in more detail the emotional root of each type and how these patterns show up in your creative life. It also goes deeper into the procrastination blends and the common reasons why writers procrastinate, giving you a more complete overall understanding of this writer's curse.

Also, if you've already taken the quiz, you don't have to retake it unless you want to. Feel free to skip ahead to your type's chapter and start working from there. But if you're curious to see how your answers might land a second time—especially now that you're more aware of your patterns—you're welcome to revisit it.

Whether this is your first step or your next step, I feel confident that once you understand procrastination and how it's affecting you a little bit better, you'll have an easier time overcoming it.

Let's get started!

# how to use this workbook

This workbook isn't here to add more pressure, but to help you relax and exhale. It's purpose is to give you space, structure, and encouragement as you move from procrastination into creative momentum.

I created it with the hope of giving you a sense of relief, like sitting down with a guide who knows what it's like to struggle with procrastination and who wants to help you take gentle, doable steps toward something better.

Most of the exercises included here are light, creative, and even fun. You won't be asked to overhaul your entire life. You'll just be invited to try new things, experiment with new thoughts, and get to know the writing version of yourself that's been trying to emerge all along.

## SO WHERE DO YOU BEGIN?

Start by taking the full quiz in the next section—unless you've already taken it in the main book and feel confident about your results.

Once you know your primary procrastination type(s), flip to the chapter that corresponds to your strongest score. That's your starting point.

Each type chapter includes:

- A description of how this pattern tends to show up in a writer's life
- A set of mindset shifts specific to this pattern
- Interactive exercises and reflection prompts
- Practical tools to help you move through the pattern
- Creative activities to get you writing again
- A planning section to keep you moving gently forward

If you identify with more than one type, that's completely normal. Many writers do. After working through your primary type, move on to any secondary or tertiary types that also resonate. You'll likely find some overlap, but also new insights, angles, or equally useful tools.

As you explore your blended types, feel free to pick and choose the exercises that speak to you. You might combine activities or revisit certain tips as your awareness deepens. There's no wrong order, and no "perfect" pace.

## DON'T SKIP THE FINAL CHAPTERS

At the end of the workbook, you'll find several bonus sections created for all procrastination types. These include support for blended identities, troubleshooting setbacks, and strengthening your momentum over time. They're designed to help you build resilience for the long haul, and remind you that change isn't linear. Some days will feel easy. Some won't. That's okay.

## WHAT THIS WORKBOOK IS REALLY ABOUT

Think of this workbook as a toolbox to return to again and again. You'll find tips, techniques, mindset shifts, prompts, challenges, and more, all designed to support your transformation from a stuck, overwhelmed, or avoidant writer into one who shows up with confidence and creative joy. This is your escape from the web. And every page is a strand you're gently unraveling. (Yeah, I like the web analogies!)

### WHAT'S CALLING YOU BACK?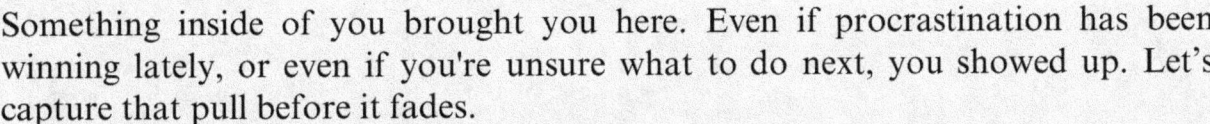

Something inside of you brought you here. Even if procrastination has been winning lately, or even if you're unsure what to do next, you showed up. Let's capture that pull before it fades.

**Step 1: Write down the moment you knew you needed to do something about your writing procrastination.** What happened? What thought wouldn't go away? What dream felt too impossible, and what made you want to reach for it again?

_____

**Step 2: Finish this sentence: "I want to write because…"** Try not to overthink it. Let it spill out. Explore different endings if you like.

_____

**Step 3: Look over your answers.** Circle the one that hits you the hardest—the one that makes you ache or smile or want to close the book and go write.

_____

**Step 4: Complete this phrase on a sticky note or scrap of paper:** "Even when I procrastinate, I still care about writing because…"

_____

Tape this note somewhere visible—your laptop. mirror, or wall. Let it remind you why you're here.

# take the quiz

# discover your 🔍 procrastination type(s)

**What if your procrastination is a pattern trying to tell you something?**

Before we can shift how you write, we need to understand what's been stopping you, not just on the surface, but at the root.

This quiz is designed to help you identify your unique procrastination pattern—or more likely, patterns. Procrastination doesn't look the same for everyone. Some writers delay because they're afraid of failure. Others avoid writing because they're exhausted, overwhelmed, distracted, or chasing perfection.

This is the full quiz featured in *Escape the Writer's Web*. If you've already taken it and feel confident in your results, you're welcome to skip ahead to your type chapters and start working through those.

But if you'd like to retake it—with fresh eyes and a deeper understanding—go right ahead. You may find that your blend has shifted, or that a secondary type speaks louder now than it did before.

This quiz isn't a test. It's a tool. Treat it with curiosity, not judgment. Answer as honestly as you can. You'll find simple scoring instructions and brief type descriptions at the end to help guide your next steps.

Keep in mind that you should respond as honestly as possible, based on who you are right now—not who you'd like to be or wish you were. In other words, don't answer as your "ideal self," but as your true self. Try to be as objective as possible, viewing yourself from the outside based on what you typically "do" rather than what you wish you'd do or think you should do.

At the same time, resist the urge to overthink your answers, as that can skew your results. Move through the questions steadily, answering without too much delay. If you're unsure, simply go with your best guess. **The quiz should take you no more than about 15 minutes.**

Let's start untangling!

# quiz

For each statement, rate how much it applies to you on a scale of 1 to 5.

1. Never
2. Rarely
3. Sometimes
4. Often
5. Always

1. ____I feel anxious and uncomfortable when starting new tasks.

2. ____I enjoy thinking about new projects more than actually working on them.

3. ____I like to make my work as good as possible before finishing it.

4. ____When faced with a task or deadline, I feel an urge to rebel against it, even if I know it's important.

5. ____I easily get distracted by other things when I'm working.

6. ____When I don't finish things as quickly as I'd like, I tend to feel bad about myself.

7. ____I find it challenging to organize my tasks and priorities.

8. ____I frequently feel too tired to work on my tasks—even if they're important.

9. ____I often doubt my ability to do tasks well, making me hesitate to work on them.

10. ____I spend a lot of time analyzing the pros and cons of starting a task before actually beginning.

11. ____I regularly take on too many commitments because I'm excited about new opportunities or feel obligated to do them.

12. ____I like to challenge rules and instructions, preferring to find my own way rather than following guidelines.

13. ____I feel more energized and motivated when the deadline is approaching.

14. ____It's common for me to get drawn into fun activities when I should be working.

15. ____When it's time to work on a writing-related task, I frequently get stuck thinking about "what if" scenarios that prevent me from actually writing or doing the work.

16. ____I find it hard to stay focused on one thing at a time.

17. ____I love brainstorming new ideas but don't always follow through with them.

18. ____When I have a deadline, I tend to feel overwhelmed and stressed.

19. ____I often feel like I don't have enough energy to get going on a writing task.

20. ____I find it hard to create and stick to a plan for my projects.

21. ____I tend to procrastinate on tasks simply because I don't like being told what to do.

22. ____I feel bad about myself for procrastinating.

23. ____I'm likely to leave projects until the last minute to create a sense of urgency.

24. ____I keep tweaking my work to make it perfect, which delays finishing it.

25. ____The main reason I procrastinate on my writing projects is because I prefer to do fun things.

26. ____I procrastinate because I think if I finish a project, I'll have to face criticism or judgment.

27. ____I sometimes feel overwhelmed by all the commitments I've made.

28. ____It's common for me to worry about making mistakes when working on a writing project.

29. ____Sometimes, I catch myself feeling badly about how I should have worked on my project much earlier or gotten more done by now.

30. ____I struggle with managing my energy levels throughout the day.

31. ____I frequently lose track of my important tasks or deadlines.

32. ____I spend too much time analyzing options before making a decision.

33. ____I delay completing projects because I want to prove that I can succeed on my own terms.

34. ____I often feel other people's work is better than mine, no matter how hard I try.

35. ____I usually get busy with a task only when the deadline is near or when I run out of more enjoyable things to do.

36. ____I tend to feel my work is never good enough.

37. ____I rarely work on something until I have a sudden burst of inspiration.

38. ____I regularly underestimate the time required to complete a task.

39. ____I get a lot done, but often, the tasks I complete are not as important to me as those I don't finish.

40. ____It usually takes me several attempts to get started working on a project.

41. ____Usually, my guilt about not working on tasks sooner is what finally inspires me to action.

42. ____I overcomplicate simple tasks by thinking too much about them.

43. ____When I imagine working on a project, I often delay because I worry I'll mess it up.

44. ____When someone imposes a deadline or expectation on me, I sometimes intentionally push back or delay to assert my independence.

45. ____I rarely get serious about working on a task until I'm in a panic about it.

46. ____I may start working on a task, but if something more fun comes up, I'll go do that instead.

47. ____I usually find that it takes me longer to complete a project than I thought it would because I get distracted along the way.

48. ____I struggle to keep my workspace and projects organized.

49. ____I often feel like I need a nap or a break before I can work on my project.

50. ____I frequently feel overwhelmed by my schedule, making it hard to prioritize and work on important projects.

51. ____I usually wait to start a task until the last possible moment.

52. ____I delay starting projects because I want everything to be just right.

53. ____If I do complete a task, my thoughts are already focused on my next big idea.

54. ____I tend to think about what could go wrong instead of taking action.

55. ____Finishing a task isn't exciting to me—it's usually just something I have to get done.

56. ____When faced with a boring task, I typically handle it by multitasking.

57. ____After completing a task, I usually feel relieved, but I also feel shame or regret for procrastinating.

58. ____I often put off tasks because I feel physically or mentally drained.

59. ____I sometimes resist tasks or responsibilities, even if they align with my personal goals, because they come with external pressure.

60. ____I like working on lists, charts, and graphs to think through a project, which often stops me from getting anything done on the project itself.

61. ____I rarely start working on my most important projects—my "dream" writing projects—until I've cleared other urgent tasks off my calendar.

62. ____I often seek reassurance from others before I feel comfortable moving forward with my task.

63. ____I struggle to turn my creative ideas into actionable steps, so they often stay in the "idea" stage.

64. ____I have high standards and aim for perfection in all my tasks.

65. ____When I finish a task, I'm actually surprised I did it on time.

66. ____I struggle with organizing new projects and often feel unsure of where to begin.

67. ____After I start a project, I often find it hard to concentrate because I'm feeling tired or sluggish.

68. ____It's common for me to delay working on writing tasks—even if they're important to me—because I have too many other commitments.

69. ____When I'm working on a project, I'll abandon it if another great idea occurs to me.

70. ____I worry excessively about failing or not living up to expectations.

71. ____I put off starting tasks to avoid feeling controlled or constrained by external demands or expectations.

72. ____When planning a project, usually what I focus on most is how I'll reward myself when it's done.

73. ____I try to focus when working on a project, but I get easily sidetracked.

74. ____I often beat myself up for not being more productive.

75. ____Sometimes, after I start working on a task, a thought occurs to me, and 30 minutes later, I'm still thinking about or examining that thought in some way.

76. ____I frequently put off tasks that make me feel anxious or uncomfortable.

77. ____I spend a lot of time on minor details to ensure everything is perfect.

78. ____When faced with multiple tasks, I prioritize the ones with the nearest deadline.

79. ____I often intend to work on a project and find an hour later that I've spent the time organizing my thoughts and/or workspace.

80. ____I frequently second-guess my decisions, causing delays in my work.

81. ____I often say, "I'll do it later," because I'd rather enjoy myself now.

82. ____It's common for me to delay starting a project because I'm just not feeling up to it energy-wise.

83. ____I frequently find myself saying, "I'll get to it when I have time," but then that time never seems to come because I have so much to do.

84. ____I'm likely to hold off on submitting a project because I'm worried it's not perfect yet.

85. ____I often feel like an imposter as a writer.

86. ____I frequently check my phone and social media when I'm supposed to be focused on a task.

87. ____When I procrastinate, I feel like I'm letting myself and/or others down.

88. ____I often delay working on a project because I'm overanalyzing the steps involved.

89. ____I usually don't start work on a project until I finally get everything organized.

90. ____I'm more likely to finish a task when I'm under time pressure to do it (when the deadline is looming).

91. ____I prefer getting lost in daydreams about future projects instead of working on current tasks.

## note from the author

*Hey, just wanted to say thank you for taking the time to do this. I know how easy it would be to flip past this section or put it off for "later." But you didn't. You're doing the work. You're not just naming the problem—you're showing up for your writing self. And it's going to lead somewhere. I can't wait for you to meet the part of yourself that already knows how to move forward. Let's check out your results!*

## answer totals

Add up your scores for the following groups of questions. For example, if you answered "3" for question #1, you would put "3" next to the corresponding question number below. Then add up your total for each row.

**Type 1:** 1___ 18___28___ 45___ 54___70___ 80___ TOTAL: ___

**Type 2:** 9___ 26___34___ 43___ 62___76___ 85___ TOTAL: ___

**Type 3:** 2___ 17___37___ 53___ 63___69___ 91___ TOTAL: ___

**Type 4:** 14___ 25___35___ 46___ 55___72___ 81___ TOTAL: ___

**Type 5:** 3___ 24___36___ 52___ 64___77___ 84___ TOTAL: ___

**Type 6:** 13___ 23___ 38___ 51___65___ 78___ 90___TOTAL: ___

**Type 7:** 5___ 16___40___ 47___ 56___73___ 86___ TOTAL: ___

**Type 8:** 11___ 27___39___ 50___ 61___68___ 83___ TOTAL: ___

**Type 9:** 6___ 22___29___ 41___ 57___74___ 87___ TOTAL: ___

**Type 10:** 7___ 20___31___ 48___ 66___79___ 89___ TOTAL: ___

**Type 11:** 10___ 15___32___ 42___ 60___75___ 88___ TOTAL: ___

**Type 12:** 8___ 19___30___ 49___ 58___67___ 82___ TOTAL: ___

**Type 13:** 4___ 12___21___ 33___ 44___59___ 71___ TOTAL: ___

In which row was your total the highest? Identify your top three in order. If you had two or more with the same totals, record all numbers in which you had the second-highest number and then all numbers in which you had the third-highest number. For example, a simple test result might look like this:

1. Score: 31—Type: 11
2. Score: 27—Type: 9
3. Score: 17—Type: 5

Your top three types would be:
1. Type 11
2. Type 9
3. Type 5

If your results had some numbers with the same totals, it may look like this:
1. Score: 31—Types: 11 and 13
2. Score: 27—Types: 9, 10, and 12
3. Score: 17—Type: 5

Your top three types would be:
1. Type 11
2. Type 13
3. Types 9, 10, and 12

You can see above that we took your top score and applied that to your top two types. They aren't in any particular order—both types are equally strong for you. Your third type is one or perhaps all three of those you had in second place with a score of 27. As you read through the types, you can determine which of those three is likely the strongest. If they are equally strong, explore all three to see what solutions may help you.

## how much does procrastination affect you?

Most writers procrastinate to some degree, but the intensity varies from person to person. Some will find that only their top two types are at play on a consistent basis. Others will discover that the problem weaves its way into their writing world more pervasively.

In my research with authors and the 13 types, I've found one key takeaway: **If you have a score of 20 or higher in any type, pay attention to it.** Read the chapter for all of those types, not just your top two or three.

Your highest-scoring types are likely to affect you the most, but I've seen authors score over 20 in multiple types. Then, when they describe their struggles with procrastination, I can hear how it manifests in different ways, often reflecting characteristics from several types.

In other words, don't limit yourself. If three or more types have a score of 20 or higher, assume that all of them are influencing your writing on some level. In Chapter 18, we'll discuss your "procrastination blend"—how your various types interact to undermine your efforts.

If only your top one or two types had scores of 20 or higher, you're likely affected primarily by those types and not as much by others that had scores of less than 20 (though some writers still reported scores of 19 as being significant).

Another thing to consider: If all of your scores are 19 or below, you're probably a "mild" procrastinator, with the issue surfacing only occasionally in your writing life. A score of 25 or higher in any type may indicate a more moderate or severe form of procrastination—you can assess that based on your own experience.

Again, this shows that we are all very different in how we experience procrastination. We differ in:

- **How much we're affected:** Some of us have trouble only occasionally, others more often, and still others struggle with it on a more consistent basis.
- **How many types:** Some of us battle with only one or two types of procrastination, while others may be affected by three, four, or more.

My goal is to help you understand exactly how procrastination affects you in your own unique way. Then, I hope to guide you in making small changes that will enable you to reach your goals without procrastination holding you back.

# procrastination types

Find all thirteen procrastination types, along with their abbreviated descriptions, below. This will give you a first glimpse into what might be happening with your particular type(s) of procrastination. When you're ready, turn to the corresponding chapters for more details, insights, and potential solutions—each type has its own dedicated chapter.

**Type 1: The Worrier**
The Worrier becomes trapped in a cycle of anxiety and overthinking, making it difficult for them to start or finish tasks. Their mind races with fears and doubts, often leaving them feeling overwhelmed by deadlines and expectations. This inner turmoil prevents them from fully tapping into their creative potential.

**Type 2: The Avoider**
The Avoider shies away from tasks due to a deep-seated fear of failure and criticism. Rather than tackling their responsibilities, they seek distractions and comfort, often leaving important projects unfinished. Procrastination becomes a way to shield themselves from potential disappointment.

**Type 3: The Dreamer**
The Dreamer is brimming with creative ideas and visions but struggles to turn them into reality. Their imagination runs wild, often causing them to get lost in thoughts rather than taking action. This lack of focus leads to many unfinished projects as they jump from one idea to the next without committing.

**Type 4: The Fun Seeker**
The Fun Seeker prioritizes pleasure and excitement over responsibilities, which frequently leads to procrastination on important tasks. They thrive on spontaneity and entertainment, making it difficult to stay focused on writing. Their carefree attitude often results in last-minute scrambling to complete tasks.

**Type 5: The Perfectionist**
The Perfectionist is driven by an intense desire for excellence, which can paralyze them when it comes to completing their writing tasks. They worry their work won't meet their high standards, leading to endless revisions and delays. This relentless pursuit of perfection often leaves them feeling frustrated and stuck.

**Type 6: The Crisis-Maker**
The Crisis-Maker thrives on the adrenaline of working under pressure, frequently putting off tasks until the final hour. While they believe they work best in the heat of the moment, this approach often leads to stress and chaos as deadlines loom. Their creative process is a whirlwind, but the results can be haphazard.

**Type 7: The Distracted**
The Distracted individual finds it challenging to focus due to a constant barrage of interruptions and temptations. Social media, entertainment, and other distractions can easily pull them away from their work. As a result, they struggle to make meaningful progress on their projects.

**Type 8: The Overdoer**
The Overdoer fills their schedule with numerous tasks and commitments, leaving little room for creative work. They thrive on staying active but often feel overwhelmed by their responsibilities, making it difficult to prioritize their writing. This constant busyness can lead to procrastination on important projects.

### Type 9: The Guilty

The Guilty type often feels weighed down by regret and self-criticism over their procrastination. They struggle with feelings of inadequacy and guilt for not being productive, often leading to a cycle of avoidance. Their desire to meet high expectations can make it difficult for them to take action.

### Type 10: The Disorganized

The Disorganized type often has a chaotic workspace and lacks structure in their creative process. This disarray makes it difficult for them to focus or find what they need, leading to procrastination. Their creativity is vibrant, but it frequently gets lost in the clutter.

### Type 11: The Overthinker

The Overthinker gets caught up in a loop of excessive analysis, preventing them from taking action. They mull over every detail, worrying about making the wrong choice. This tendency often leads to delays and a lack of productivity.

### Type 12: The Tired

The Tired type often struggles with fatigue, making it difficult to find the motivation and energy for their creative projects. They may long to engage with their writing but wrestle with brain fog, exhaustion, or insomnia, making it hard to bring their full attention to the page when it's time.

### Type 13: The Defier

The Defier thrives on rebellion and challenges conventional expectations, which can lead to procrastination. They have a strong desire for creative freedom, but their resistance to structure can leave projects incomplete or cause their stories to lack forward momentum. Their journey involves striking a balance between independence and productivity.

# after the quiz: what's next?

You've completed the quiz and discovered your type—or your unique blend of types. Now it's time to explore what that actually means in your writing life. In the chapters ahead, you'll find a dedicated section for each of the 13 procrastination types, packed with tools, mindset shifts, exercises, and creative challenges tailored to that pattern.

Start with your strongest-scoring type—the one that shows up most consistently in your writing behavior. Then move on to any other types that scored high or rang true for you. Each chapter can be used independently or in combination with others.

You may find yourself nodding in recognition. You may feel a little called out. Either way, you're not here to be perfect. You're here to get free and get back to writing!

# name your inner creative voice

Before you dive into your type chapter, let's meet the part of you that still believes in this writing thing. This is the part that never really gives up, no matter how tangled the web gets. It might be hidden right now... or tired... or a little afraid. But it's still there. Let's bring it into the light.

We're going to give that inner creative voice a name. Remember, we're not talking about your inner critic or perfectionist, but the you who wants to create, even if it's messy or no one sees it. Even if it takes a really long time.

**Need help naming this voice? Try these prompts:**

- **If your creative voice had a superpower, what would it be?** (Hope? Courage? Curiosity? Finishing even when the words aren't flowing?)
- **If it showed up in your life as a guide or character, what would it look like?** (A sparkly librarian? A chaotic inventor? A soft-spoken time traveler?)
- **What energy do you want your writing life to have?** (Steady? Bold? Mysterious? Sacred? Joyful?)
- **What name would make you smile when you hear it?** (It can be serious or silly. Whatever reminds you: I'm still a writer.)

**Now try this:**

Write your inner creative voice's name below. Then describe it—or draw it if you like.

My inner creative voice is named: _____

It is... (funny? soft-spoken? endlessly curious? always scribbling ideas on napkins?)

_____

# the procrastination types

# meet the worrier

**You hesitate to write, imagining every potential mistake before you begin.**

You want to write, but something always feels off. Maybe you're not quite ready, the idea hasn't fully clicked, or you're still working on your outline. You tell yourself you're preparing. And you are, but you're also protecting yourself.

As a Worrier, your procrastination is often rooted in anxiety. You might be nervous about starting something you can't finish, afraid your work won't be good enough, or concerned about what others might think. So you delay, often because it feels safer to wait than to risk doing it "wrong."

Unfortunately, the more this happens, the more waiting becomes a pattern in your writing life. Worse, the longer you delay, the harder it becomes to restart the project you were working on. In this section, you'll learn how to recognize your patterns and gently step out of them.

## COMMON TRAITS OF A WORRIER WRITER

- Feel afraid to start a new project for fear you'll mess it up.
- Try to anticipate every problem before you proceed.
- Obsess over whether something is "the right" idea or path.
- Avoid feedback out of fear of criticism.
- Rewrite the same sections multiple times without moving forward.
- Delay finishing because then you'd have to share or release it.
- Worry about making mistakes or disappointing others.

## SELF-CHECK: DO YOU RECOGNIZE THIS PATTERN?

Check all that apply:
- ☐ I often delay starting a project because I'm not sure I'm ready.
- ☐ I tend to research, plan, or outline instead of writing actual words.
- ☐ I often worry about making mistakes when facing a blank page.
- ☐ I get stuck rewriting the same section to make it "just right."
- ☐ I frequently avoid sharing my work because I'm afraid it's full of mistakes.
- ☐ I worry that once I finish, I'll realize it's not good enough.
- ☐ I often listen to my inner critic about how "bad" my writing is.

# worry-breaker matrix

Whenever you feel your inner Worrier dragging you down into research spirals, perfection paralysis, or that familiar "I'm not ready" loop, come back to this matrix. Scan down the rows and across the columns for the description that best matches your stuck moment, then immediately do the tiny, paired action beside it. Don't overthink it: set a timer if needed, do the micro-move, then celebrate your progress.

| When I catch myself... | I will... |
|---|---|
| Over-researching | Write one messy sentence right now. |
| Over-planning | Set a 10-minute timer and just start drafting. |
| Obsessively rewriting | Draft an entirely new paragraph without editing. |
| Seeking absolute certainty | Freewrite for 5 minutes—no questions asked. |
| Afraid to make mistakes | Journal about one fear for 2 minutes, then write. |
| Avoiding the first draft | Open my document and write a single sentence. |
| Hunting perfect words | Close my browser and jot down 100 words. |
| In a self-doubt freeze | Share one sentence with a trusted friend. |
| Endlessly outlining | Bullet-list my next three scenes in 3 minutes. |

 **JOURNAL PROMPT**

Where does this fear of "not being ready" show up most in your writing process? Is it when starting? Finishing? Sharing?

# shift your writing mindset

**You don't need full certainty to begin. Action breeds confidence.**

When you're a Worrier, your mindset is often focused on avoiding danger, failure, or judgment. You might think, "If I wait until I'm sure, nothing bad will happen." But that mindset keeps you stuck. Changing your mindset doesn't mean ignoring your fears. It means retraining your inner voice to focus on progress, resilience, and trust so you can move forward.

## MINDSET REFRAME #1

**Old mindset:** "If I plan enough, I'll avoid mistakes."
**New mindset:** "Momentum reveals what planning can't."
Overplanning feels like protection, but it often becomes a fortress that keeps you from ever stepping outside. You don't have to leap into the unknown without a map; you just need to take a small step forward and let the path reveal itself.

**Reflect:**
When was the last time you planned so much that you never actually got started?

_____

What's one tiny step you could take today, just to learn what happens when you act despite uncertainty?

_____

## MINDSET REFRAME #2

**Old mindset:** "If something goes wrong, I'll be ruined."
**New mindset:** "Mistakes teach me what to try next."
When you worry, every stumble feels like proof you were wrong to even start. But each misstep actually maps the path forward. Embracing errors as clues lets you experiment without fear, turning "What if I fail?" into "What can I learn?"

**Reflect:**
If you abandoned a project at the first sign of trouble, what did you miss by stopping?

_____

Do something this week you think will fail. Whatever happens, reflect on what you learned.

_____

## QUICK ACTION

List two simple ways you'll remind yourself of these new mindsets during writing sessions (i.e., sticky notes, phone background, timer alert):

1._____

2._____

# your personal mindset reframe

Changing your mindset isn't about pretending you have no fear. The fear is still there, but you choose a new message that's strong enough to walk you through it. In the space below, you'll create your own personalized reframe. You want to speak directly to the way your inner Worrier tries to hold you back, and the way your courageous self will answer it.

## STEP 1: RECOGNIZE THE PATTERN

What is a common thought you have that leads you to delay or avoid writing?
(Example: *"I'm not ready."*)

_____

_____

## STEP 2: WRITE A MORE SUPPORTIVE TRUTH

What new thought will you practice this week to move forward anyway?
(Example: *"I'm allowed to start messy. I'll figure it out as I go."*)

_____

_____

### MY INNER COURAGE CARD

Use an index card, sticky note, or whatever you like. Write it big, decorate it, or make a small "badge" for your writing space.

**Old thought I'm replacing:** _____

**New thought I'm practicing:** _____

# my hidden rewards

**Worry feels like protection, but it slows you down.**

Even though it may feel frustrating, procrastination can also create real payoffs that your brain craves. Unfortunately, those payoffs come at a hidden cost: your growth, confidence, and writing progress. By getting honest about the real rewards procrastination is giving you—and the new rewards you truly want—you start building awareness that leads to real change.

## WHAT ARE YOUR HIDDEN REWARDS?

Which of these rewards resonate with you? (Check all that apply.)

**When I avoid my writing, I might be getting:**

☐ A feeling of safety by avoiding judgment.

☐ The ability to stay in control by not risking failure.

☐ Relief from the feelings of being overwhelmed or anxious.

☐ Protection of my writing dream by never testing it in reality.

☐ An escape from hard emotions like frustration or self-doubt.

☐ Temporary relief by doing something easier.

☐ To preserve the fantasy of becoming a perfect writer someday.

Other hidden payoffs I've noticed:

_____

_____

_____

_____

 **JOURNAL PROMPT**

What have these hidden rewards been costing you creatively, emotionally, and personally?

# future payoffs

Now imagine the payoffs you'll unlock by moving forward, even imperfectly. Which future outcomes excite you most? (Check all that apply.)

**If I face the worry and show up anyway, I could gain:**

☐ Real momentum on a meaningful project.
☐ True confidence in my writing identity.
☐ Trust in myself to work through doubt or fear.
☐ A finished project that makes me feel proud.
☐ Increased creative courage with each session.
☐ Reduced anxiety around my writing.
☐ Joy in storytelling again.

## OTHER BENEFITS I WANT TO CLAIM

_____     _____

_____     _____

## "WHY I WRITE" CARD

In moments of fear or hesitation, it's easy to forget why you started writing in the first place. Creating a personal reminder of your deeper motivations helps anchor you to your real reasons for showing up. In the space below, write or design your own "Why I Write" Card. Use bullet points, sentences, quotes, or whatever speaks to you. Decorate it later if you want, and keep it where you can see it often.

WHY I WRITE

# your new writer identity

**You don't need more planning. You need courage to move forward.**

It may seem like to overcome procrastination, you just have to do things differently. But actually, it helps to imagine *becoming* someone different. When you move from "I'm a writer who always hesitates" to "I'm a writer who takes small courageous steps", you're not just building a new habit, but a new identity. This is one of the most powerful transformations you can create for yourself, because once you start seeing yourself differently, your actions naturally begin to follow.

## MY WRITING IDENTITY SHIFT

### Step 1: How do you see yourself now?
Think about the kinds of things you say to yourself when you feel stuck. Here are some common Worrier identity thoughts:

- "I'm someone who can't start until I feel 100% certain."
- "I believe any mistake will prove I'm a failure."
- "I overthink every detail so nothing ever gets done."
- "I feel I must anticipate every problem before I begin."

Now, write 3 beliefs, labels, or self-messages you often carry about yourself as a writer.

_____

_____

_____

### Step 2: Who do you want to become?
Now, imagine yourself six months from today. You've been showing up and taking small courageous steps, even when fear tried to stop you. What new self-messages would you love to carry instead? Here are some examples to inspire you:
- "I'm a writer who moves forward even when I feel uncertain."
- "I follow through on my ideas with persistence and heart."
- "I give myself permission to write messy first drafts."
- "I trust myself to figure things out as I go."

Write 3 beliefs you want to grow into.

_____

_____

_____

**Step 3: What would that version of you do next?**
Next, using the ideas you wrote down, create a simple statement that captures who you are becoming as a writer.

Try this formula:
**Even though I usually _____, I'm learning to _____.**

Here are some examples:
- Even though I usually freeze when I fear making a mistake, I'm learning to start with just one imperfect sentence.
- Even though I usually overthink every step before I begin, I'm learning to write first and refine later.
- Even though I usually wait for certainty, I'm learning to move forward with curiosity instead of guarantees.

**MY IDENTITY BRIDGE STATEMENT**

_____

_____

_____

**ENCOURAGE YOURSELF!**

**Remember:** Every small choice you make to sit down, write a messy paragraph, or move forward even when you're unsure, is a vote for the writer you're becoming. You don't have to be fearless to grow, just willing to keep showing up, one small act of courage at a time. If you can say to yourself, "What would courageous me do right now?" it might help!

*The fear hasn't gone away,*
*but I'm learning to begin*
*even with it whispering nearby.*

# tools to write through worry

**When worry strikes, use strategies to keep your words flowing.**

Worry thrives on uncertainty and fear. Fortunately, there are tools you can use to help build structures of safety and momentum so that even when anxiety pops up, you still have a way forward. Think of these tools like hiking gear: You don't need to climb the whole mountain today, you just need a sturdy handhold for your next few steps. Some tools will work better for you than others, and that's okay. Your job isn't to use them all at once. It's to experiment and discover what gives you a little more courage, breathing room, and forward momentum.

## TOOLKIT FOR THE WORRIER

### Set a 15-Minute Timer

Limit how long you spend preparing or overthinking before you begin. For example: Plan for 15 minutes, then start writing no matter what.

### Outline Only What You Need

At first, skip complex charts or deep worldbuilding. Build a simple 5-point outline to feel "safe enough" to move forward.

### Journal Your "What If" Fears

Before a writing session, spend 5 minutes writing down your worst-case scenarios. Getting them out of your head weakens their grip.

### Start Messy on Purpose

Give yourself permission to write bad sentences. Let the first draft be your exploration, not your final product.

### Create a Calming Writing Ritual

Signal safety to your mind by pairing writing with a soothing habit—tea, music, a candle, stretching, or a short walk.

### Celebrate Tiny Wins

Notice and reward even the smallest progress. For example: "I wrote one paragraph—time for a gold star sticker!"

### Build a Courage Anchor

Choose a phrase to tell yourself when fear rises. For example: "I don't have to be ready. I just have to begin."

### Your Turn!

## CHOOSE TWO TOOLS

After reviewing the toolkit, pick two strategies that feel most helpful for you right now. For each one, write a small, clear action step you'll take to practice this week. It doesn't have to be a huge plan, just one real thing you'll try.

*Examples:*

- If you choose the **15-Minute Timer** tool, your action step might be: "Set a timer for 15 minutes tomorrow and start drafting without overthinking."
- If you choose the **Journal Your What-Ifs** tool, your action step might be: "Before my next session, I'll spend 5 minutes listing my biggest fears, then write anyway."
- If you choose the **Create a Calming Ritual** tool, your action step might be: "Make tea and light a candle before I open my laptop to write."

## MY TOOLS AND ACTION STEPS

Tool #1 I'm Choosing:

_____

Action Step I'll Take:

_____

Tool #2 I'm Choosing:

_____

Action Step I'll Take:

_____

## THE WORRIER'S ANCHOR PHRASE

Worriers need a simple reminder to begin and to trust themselves as they go. Write an anchor phrase that grounds you when worry starts to spin its stories. Examples:

- "I can feel nervous and still begin."
- "I don't need certainty to take the next step."
- "It's safe to try, even if I'm unsure."

**My personal anchor phrase:**

_____

# mapping your novel journey

**You don't need perfect plans to get started.**

Big goals feel overwhelming, but small steps create momentum. Each tiny action you take builds courage, trust, and momentum, so let's use them! This week, choose three micro-steps you can realistically complete, even if they feel almost too small to matter. (They do matter. Try it and see how you feel!)

## QUICK IDEAS FOR SMALL STEPS

(Choose or modify!)

- Open your draft and reread the last paragraph.
- Brainstorm 3 possible scene ideas.
- Freewrite about your main character for 5 minutes.
- Write one messy paragraph without judging it.
- Outline the next 5 scenes (quick bullets, not perfect).
- Journal your current writing fear and how you'll move through it.
- Spend 10 minutes imagining your novel's opening setting.

## MY SMALL STEPS FOR THE WEEK

| Day | One small action... | Did I take it? |
|-----------|---------------------|----------------|
| Monday | | |
| Tuesday | | |
| Wednesday | | |
| Thursday | | |
| Friday | | |
| Saturday | | |
| Sunday | | |

# NOVEL-WRITING ROADMAP

## Step 1: Make It Feel Possible

- Choose one scene that excites you—not necessarily the opening scene.
- Set a tiny goal for your first session. ("Write 100 messy words about a character.")
- Create a no-judgment zone: Tell yourself this draft is purely for exploration.

*Examples:*
- "I'm curious about how my character meets their love interest. I'll just sketch that."
- "I'll write one paragraph describing a setting, even if I'm not sure where it fits yet."

**My make-it-possible strategy:**

_____

## Step 2: Outline in Layers

- Write a one-sentence summary of your story's idea.
- Expand to 5 major story points (beginning, middle events, climax, ending).
- Create a bare-bones scene list if needed—no fancy charts required!

*Examples:*
- Hero called to adventure | refuses | accepts | battles enemy | returns home changed.
- Scene list: Opening at marketplace → Meets mentor → First big failure → Learns hidden strength → Final confrontation.

**My layered outlines:**

_____

## Step 3: Build a Worry-Free Writing Routine

- Choose two short writing sessions per week. (15-30 minutes each is enough.)
- Celebrate effort, not word count. (Example: "I showed up. That's the win.")
- Pair writing with a comforting ritual to reduce anxiety.

*Examples:*
- Light a candle and set a timer for 20 minutes every Tuesday and Friday morning.
- Have a special "writing tea" you only drink while working.

**My worry-free routine:**

_____

# carry your courage forward

**Change your thoughts and your actions will change.**

Always remember: Worry is your brain's way of keeping you safe. But staying "safe" by procrastinating costs you the joy of building something amazing. You don't have to silence the worry, just learn to respond to with courage. Below are some common Worrier thoughts and how you can shift them into a more confident, compassionate voice.

## SHIFT YOUR SELF-TALK

| Worry Thought | Courage Reframe |
|---|---|
| "I'm not ready to start." | "I'm ready enough to take one small step." |
| "What if it's terrible?" | "It's allowed to be messy at first." |
| "I don't know enough yet." | "I'll learn what I need by moving forward." |
| "I'll never finish." | "I only need to finish today's small piece." |

**Your Turn**

Write down a worry you often hear in your mind, then answer it with a new, more courageous voice.

| Worry Thought | Courage Reframe |
|---|---|
| | |
| | |
| | |
| | |

**YOUR COURAGE PLAN**

**1. What's one small thing I want to remind myself when I feel worry rising again?**
(Example: "Starting small is still starting." Or: "I'm allowed to write before I'm ready.")

_____

**2. What's one ritual or anchor I can use to help me feel safer when I start writing?**
(Examples: tea, candle, mantra, song.)

_____

**3. What's one way I'll celebrate myself after every writing effort?**
(Examples: sticker chart, favorite snack, five minutes of stretching in the sun.)

_____

**LOOKING BACK**

Every time you shift a worry into a courageous thought, you're building trust in yourself—and trust builds momentum. The old patterns of overthinking, fear, and freezing may still threaten your progress sometimes. But now you have something new:

- Awareness of your patterns.
- Tools to navigate fear.
- A new writing identity.
- Proof that you can act even when you're worried.

Using these tools, you'll be more likely to be able to create a new courageous writer inside you. Just take it one small, brave moment at a time.

# courage commitment

*I commit to showing up for my writing, even when I feel unsure. Each small step I take builds the writer I am becoming.*

Signed: _____

Date: _____

# meet the avoider

**Avoidance is emotional self-protection.**

You think about writing. You may even talk about it. But when it comes time to act, something inside you quietly steps back. It might look like distraction, or busyness, or letting someone else's needs take precedence. But beneath all that, avoidance is often a way of shielding yourself from emotional discomfort.

Writing brings things up. It makes you vulnerable. And if you've ever been judged, misunderstood, or made to feel "not enough," it's no surprise that your mind would want to protect you from that feeling. Now, some part of you is trying to stay safe.

You may avoid finishing because finishing means sharing, or resist starting because starting makes it real. You may do everything except write because writing feels like it might expose something tender. In this chapter, we're going to help you build trust within yourself so that your writing becomes a place of freedom, not fear.

## COMMON TRAITS OF A AVOIDER WRITER

- Delay writing by telling yourself you're not ready.
- Feel safer keeping your work to yourself.
- Drop projects as they start to feel real or risky.
- Tell yourself "you'll get to it" later (and rarely do).
- Avoid finishing because sharing feels too vulnerable.
- Say yes to other obligations instead of your writing.
- Feel a mix of relief and regret when you skip writing.

## SELF-CHECK: DO YOU RECOGNIZE THIS PATTERN?

Check all that apply:
- ☐ I avoid writing when I think I might feel something I don't want to.
- ☐ I hold off on sharing because I don't want people to judge me.
- ☐ I pretend I'm "just too busy" when I'm really avoiding discomfort.
- ☐ I tell myself I'll write later—but later rarely arrives.
- ☐ I walk away when a project starts to feel too emotionally risky.
- ☐ I feel like it's safer not to try than to try and fail.
- ☐ I feel a quiet ache when I think about the writing I'm not doing.

# avoidance-buster matrix

Use this grid whenever you find yourself making excuses, deciding you're "too busy," or hiding from your writing. Find the row that best describes your stuck moment, then do the paired micro-action immediately. Don't overthink it, just interrupt the avoidance with a tiny step forward.

| Avoidance cue... | Immediate action |
|---|---|
| You're busy with "important" but irrelevant tasks. | Close all tabs, open your draft, and write one sentence. No editing allowed. |
| You're suddenly "not in the mood" to start. | Set a 5-minute timer and freewrite whatever comes to mind. |
| You're making excuses ("I need more research"). | Pick one question that relates to your project, write a quick answer in 2 minutes, then stop. |
| You hesitate to share because you fear criticism. | Copy one paragraph and send it to a trusted friend. Ask for one good comment about it. |
| You "have to" clean/tidy your workspace before writing. | Grab your notebook (or blank doc) and sketch three scene ideas. |
| You decide you'll write "later." | Open your project and write two words. If you want to keep going, do! |

**JOURNAL PROMPT**
**When does writing start to feel emotionally risky for you?**
Is it starting? Finishing? Sharing? What emotions might you be avoiding, and how do you protect yourself from them?

# shift your writing mindset

**You can protect yourself and progress at the same time.**

As an Avoider, your mind may be trying to keep you safe, but safe doesn't always mean fulfilled. Often, it means you feel stuck or like your writing dreams will never come true. A simple mindset shift can help you see things differently. These reframes will guide you through discomfort without abandoning your voice.

## MINDSET REFRAME #1

**Old mindset:** "If I don't try, I can't fail."
**New mindset:** "Trying is how I learn what I'm capable of."
Avoidance feels like protection, but it often robs you of your best discoveries. By not trying, you may avoid disappointment, but you also avoid connection, progress, and the deep satisfaction of growing into the writer you want to be. You don't have to push yourself into big risks. Taking small steps where you try something just to see where it leads can show you strength you didn't know you had.

**Reflect:**
When was the last time you avoided trying something you really wanted to do?

_____

What small thing might you try now—not to prove anything, but to learn something about yourself?

_____

## MINDSET REFRAME #2

**Old mindset:** "It's safer to keep this to myself."
**New mindset:** "My words deserve to be heard when I'm ready to share them."
As an Avoider, sharing may feel like exposure. To help yourself overcome the fear, practice thinking of your work as something worthy of being seen. Imagine it as something that might help, inspire, or move someone else. You can choose how and when to share, but don't let fear be the only influence on that choice.

**Reflect:**
What's one piece of writing you've kept hidden because you don't feel ready?

_____

Can you think of one small way to share your work that you can try this week?

_____

## QUICK ACTION

Choose one small writing task this week that feels emotionally safe, but still moves you forward. (Examples: reread a scene, write for five minutes, open your file and name what you feel, write and publish a blog or social media post.)

_____

# your personal mindset reframe

Sometimes, the hardest part of writing is simply allowing yourself to begin, especially when fear or discomfort makes you want to pull back. Let's try writing a new message to yourself: Use the space below to create a mindset reframe that fits your version of avoidance and what helps you move through it.

### STEP 1: RECOGNIZE THE PATTERN

What do you usually tell yourself when you're avoiding your writing?
(Example: "I'll get to it later," or "It's just not the right time.")

_____

_____

### STEP 2: WRITE A MORE SUPPORTIVE TRUTH

Try writing a new message to yourself—one that's gentle, honest, and rooted in trust rather than fear.
(Example: "I can write even if I'm unsure," or "I don't need to share this yet, but I will find a way to do so that feels manageable.")

_____

_____

 **MY INNER TRUST CARD**
Use an index card, sticky note, or whatever you like. Write it big, decorate it, or make a small "badge" for your writing space.

**Old thought I'm replacing:** _____

**New thought I'm practicing:** _____

# my hidden rewards

**Avoiding writing may feel safe, but freedom feels better.**

Avoidance typically comes from emotion, and emotions can be powerful motivators, even when they're working against us. In this way, procrastination often offers hidden payoffs. You may not notice them at first, but your brain is getting something out of the pattern. It could be relief, protection, reduced anxiety, or permission not to feel exposed. This section will help you recognize what you're getting from avoidance, and what you could gain by moving through it.

## WHAT ARE YOUR HIDDEN REWARDS?

**When I avoid my writing, I might be getting:** (check all that apply)

☐ Temporary relief from self-doubt.

☐ A way to avoid emotional discomfort or past pain.

☐ Protection from the fear of being judged.

☐ Time to do things that feel safer or more familiar.

☐ Permission to focus on others instead of myself.

☐ A sense of control in a process that feels vulnerable.

☐ Distance from something that scares me (success, failure, exposure).

Other hidden payoffs I've noticed:

_____

_____

_____

_____

**JOURNAL PROMPT**

What have these hidden rewards been costing you—creatively, emotionally, personally?

# future payoffs

Now let's look at what you could gain by gently moving through avoidance instead of staying stuck in it. Which future outcomes excite you most? (Check all that apply.)

**If I face the discomfort and show up anyway, I could gain:**

☐ A deeper sense of self-trust.
☐ Creative momentum and clarity.
☐ Relief from the guilt of not writing.
☐ A stronger connection with my writing voice.
☐ Emotional strength from facing what I used to avoid.
☐ Confidence from completing something important.
☐ Freedom to write without second-guessing every step.

## OTHER BENEFITS I WANT TO CLAIM

_____    _____

_____    _____

## "WHY I WRITE" CARD

In moments of fear or hesitation, it's easy to forget why you started writing in the first place. Creating a personal reminder of your deeper motivations helps anchor you to your real reasons for showing up. In the space below, write or design your own "Why I Write" Card. Use bullet points, sentences, quotes, or whatever speaks to you. Decorate it later if you want, and keep it where you can see it often.

WHY I WRITE

# your new writer identity

**Let's create a new story about who you really are.**

If you keep trying to write the way you have before, you'll likely fall into the same avoidance cycle because you're still carrying the identity that made avoidance feel necessary. Avoidance isn't just an action. It reflects how you see yourself. It says: "I'm someone who pulls back when it gets too real." Or, "I don't follow through." But you don't have to keep living by that version of you. Try asking: Who do I want to become? Because when your identity shifts, your choices do too.

## MY WRITING IDENTITY SHIFT

### Step 1: How do you see yourself now?

What do you tend to think about yourself as a writer when you're avoiding your work? Here are some common Avoider identity thoughts:

- "I'm someone who disappears when writing gets uncomfortable."
- "I can't handle the emotions writing brings up."
- "I hide my work because it probably isn't good enough."
- "I'm afraid that if I finish, people will expect more from me."

Now, write 3 beliefs, labels, or self-messages you often carry about yourself as a writer.

_____

_____

_____


### Step 2: Who do you want to become?

Instead of trying to "fix" yourself, try shifting your identity. Who would you be if you weren't ruled by avoidance, but guided by trust and creative honesty? Examples:

- "I'm a writer who returns, even when I've been gone awhile."
- "I face discomfort with gentleness, not avoidance."
- "I'm learning to write through the fear, not around it."
- "I share my work on my own terms, and that's enough."

Write 3 beliefs you want to grow into.

_____

_____

_____

**Step 3: What would that version of you do next?**
Now try writing a sentence that connects your old pattern with the new writer you're becoming.

Try this formula:
**Even though I usually _____, I'm learning to _____.**

Here are some examples:
- Even though I usually shut down when writing feels emotional, I'm learning to stay with it for a few minutes longer.
- Even though I usually keep my work to myself, I'm learning to trust that my voice deserves to be heard.
- Even though I usually tell myself "later," I'm learning to show up, even if it's just for five minutes.

## MY IDENTITY BRIDGE STATEMENT

_____

_____

_____

## ENCOURAGE YOURSELF!

**Remember:** You don't need to become someone completely different. But you do need to stop vanishing when things get hard. The real shift happens when you choose to stay just a little longer rather than disappear. Each time you show up, you reinforce a new story: That you are the kind of writer who moves through discomfort, not around it.

> # The difficult emotions may still be there, but I'm learning to show up, even when it feels hard.

# tools to write past avoidance

**When your emotions rise up, use tools to keep moving forward.**

When you're dealing with difficult emotions, it can be tough to resist them. Using the right tools can help you return to your writing even when avoidance is tempting you to procrastinate. Your challenge isn't always getting the words down but choosing to stay emotionally present when writing starts to feel uncomfortable.

These tools are meant to support you so you can gently re-engage instead of retreating. Try them. Tweak them. Make them yours.

## TOOLKIT FOR THE AVOIDER

### The 3-Minute Window

Set a timer for just three minutes and do anything related to your writing. Open your file, skim a paragraph, jot a note. This is about entry, not accomplishment.

### Label the Emotion

When you feel like avoiding, pause and name what you're feeling. Is it fear? Shame? Self-doubt? Naming it helps reduce its power.

### Write the Resistance

Start your session by writing about why you don't want to write. Let it all out. Often, that clears the fog and lets you move forward.

### Soften the Task

Break your writing goal into something gentler. Instead of "Write chapter 3," try "Explore the next scene." Shift from pressure to play.

### Create a Landing Ritual

Choose one calming action that tells your brain, "It's writing time." Light a candle, make tea, stretch, etc. Just keep it simple and repeatable.

### Affirm Your Return

Repeat a short sentence to yourself before you begin: "I can return to this." Or, "I don't need to be perfect to begin." Say it like you mean it.

### Check Your Avoidance Voice

Notice the moment your mind offers an escape ("Just scroll for a minute..."). Instead of obeying it, write down what it said. Then write one sentence on your story anyway.

### Your Turn!

## CHOOSE TWO TOOLS

After reviewing the toolkit, pick two strategies that feel most helpful for you right now. For each one, write a small, clear action step you'll take to practice this week. This doesn't have to be a huge plan. Just set up one real thing you'll try.

*Examples:*

- If you chose **The 3-Minute Window,** your action step might be: "Set a timer for 3 minutes and freewrite whatever I'm feeling."
- If you chose **Label the Emotion**, your action might be: "Pause before writing and name what I'm feeling on paper."
- If you chose **Create a Landing Ritual**, your step could be: "Light a candle before opening my manuscript to signal that it's time to write."

## MY TOOLS AND ACTION STEPS

Tool #1 I'm Choosing:

_____

Action Step I'll Take:

_____

Tool #2 I'm Choosing:

_____

Action Step I'll Take:

_____

## THE AVOIDER'S AFFIRMATION

Avoiders may not always realize when their emotions are getting the upper hand. Write a mantra or phrase that helps when you're tempted to avoid your writing. Examples:

- "This doesn't have to feel easy to matter."
- "I can stay with myself for one more moment."
- "I know my voice matters, even if I'm not sure it does in the moment."

**My personal affirmation:**

_____

# mapping your novel journey

**Show up for 7 days, even if it's just for five minutes a day.**

Avoiders tend to disappear when things get uncomfortable, especially when the goal feels too big. That's why daily follow-through matters. It's not about writing for hours, but proving to yourself that you can keep returning. Use this 7-day planner to track one specific, simple writing-related action each day.

## QUICK IDEAS FOR SMALL STEPS

(Choose or modify!)

- Write a single sentence that expresses how your character feels.
- Add one line of dialogue to your current scene.
- Choose one writing decision you've been avoiding and make a rough call (even if you change it later).
- Freewrite for five minutes without stopping—no filtering, no fixing.
- Open a draft and revise just the first paragraph.
- Make a list of messy ideas for your next scene. No editing allowed.

## MY SMALL STEPS FOR THE WEEK

| Day | One small action... | Did I take it? |
|---|---|---|
| **Monday** | | |
| **Tuesday** | | |
| **Wednesday** | | |
| **Thursday** | | |
| **Friday** | | |
| **Saturday** | | |
| **Sunday** | | |

## NOVEL-WRITING ROADMAP

### Step 1: Know Where You're Headed
Instead of walking away, create a gentle compass for your story.

- Write a one-sentence version of your ending, even if it changes later.
- Choose one emotional beat you want your character to hit.
- Describe what you want the reader to feel when they finish the book.
- Write a note to your future self: Here's why this story matters to me.

**My plan-ahead strategy:**

_____

### Step 2: Break It Down Before You Burn Out

- One sentence per scene; one beat per chapter.
- One journal entry from your main character's POV.
- One small writing session per week (not per day).

_Examples:_
- "This week, I'll explore just the midpoint scene without pressure to finish it."
- "I'll write one sentence of emotional subtext per scene."
- "I'll name the 3 most emotionally charged scenes so I can prepare for them."

**My break-it-down action:**

_____

### Step 3: Plan for Avoidance Before It Shows Up
You already know your pattern. So instead of blaming yourself when it happens again, plan for it. Create a soft re-entry strategy for when you ghost your project.

_Examples:_
- Keep a sticky note on your desktop that says: "Just read one line."
- Create a 3-minute "return ritual" you can use after time away.
- Write a short reminder to your future self: It's okay to start again.

**My avoidance plan:**

_____

# carry your bravery forward

**Bravery grows every time you show up anyway.**

Avoiders know the nudge to hide at the first sign of discomfort. But each time you respond with a small act of bravery—like opening the document, sharing a snippet, or moving forward despite the fear—you weaken the old avoidance habit and strengthen your new "Brave Creator" identity. You don't have to banish every fear. Just gradually change how you respond to it.

## SHIFT YOUR SELF-TALK

| Avoider Thought | Bravery Reframe |
|---|---|
| "What if they hate my work?" | "Some will connect to my creations. Others won't matter to my growth." |
| "I'm not ready to share this." | "I can share imperfect work to learn and improve." |
| "I'll feel exposed if I finish." | "I choose progress over comfort." |
| "It's safer to stay private." | "Bravery lives in small acts of vulnerability." |

### Your Turn
Write down an avoidance thought you often hear in your mind. Then answer it with a new, braver voice.

| Avoider Thought | Bravery Reframe |
|---|---|
|  |  |
|  |  |
|  |  |
|  |  |

## YOUR BRAVERY PLAN

**1. What's one small prompt I'll use when avoidance whispers?**
(e.g., "Just show one sentence.")

_____

**2. What's one quick ritual that helps me feel safe enough to start?**
(e.g., five deep breaths, a quick stretch, a favorite music track.)

_____

**3. How will I celebrate each writing effort, no matter how small?**
(e.g., check a box, a short walk, jot a "victory" note in my journal.)

_____

## LOOKING BACK

Old habits like shutting down, hiding, and succumbing to self-doubt may still mess you up sometimes. But now you've built new strengths:

- Awareness of your avoidance triggers.
- Tools to share and face fear.
- A writer identity rooted in courage.
- Proof that you can show up, even when you're scared.

Use these gifts to nurture your brave writer self one small, fearless step at a time.

# bravery commitment

*Whenever I feel afraid or uncomfortable, I commit to choosing bravery over avoidance.*

Signed: _____

Date: _____

# meet the dreamer

**You're full of ideas, but finishing feels impossible.**

You're brimming with big visions, but they rarely make it onto the page. You love the spark of a brand-new idea, yet when it comes to the slog of details, your enthusiasm quickly fades.

As a Dreamer, your imagination is both your greatest gift and your biggest roadblock. Your mind moves at lightning speed, leaping from one concept to the next, leaving projects half-done and momentum stalled. You long to bring your ideas to life, but the gap between vision and execution can feel overwhelming.

Deadlines feel too rigid and structure too limiting, so you drift, waiting for inspiration to strike again. Meanwhile, your stories stay trapped in your mind, just out of reach. With a few grounded tools and gentle structure, you can turn things around and start building a bridge between your dream and the page.

## COMMON TRAITS OF A DREAMER WRITER

- You generate concept after concept, but struggle to finish any of them.
- You picture your work as a masterpiece, making the actual writing feel insufficient.
- New ideas pull you off course before you complete the one you started.
- You write only when inspiration strikes, which means you rarely sit down to write.
- You hate wrestling with the nitty-gritty, preferring the thrill of big-picture dreaming.
- You set lofty goals but lack a step-by-step roadmap to reach them.
- You spend more time imagining the impact of your work than actually creating it.

## SELF-CHECK: DO YOU RECOGNIZE THIS PATTERN?

Check all that apply:
- ☐ I have more half-finished drafts than complete ones.
- ☐ I jump to a new idea whenever my current project gets hard.
- ☐ I believe I'll write "when the time is right"—which never comes.
- ☐ I spend more time brainstorming than drafting.
- ☐ I avoid outlining or mapping details because it feels tedious.
- ☐ I set big goals but never break them down into doable steps.
- ☐ I imagine success vividly, but rarely take the actions that make it real.

# idea-grounder matrix

Whenever your inner Dreamer pulls you into endless possibilities—like sketching future plots, brainstorming new characters, or imagining perfect outcomes—use this matrix to interrupt the cycle and pivot back into real writing. Scan down the "When I catch myself..." column and across the "Then I will..." column to find the match for your daydream detour, then jump into action.

| When I catch myself... | Then I will... |
|---|---|
| Sketching a new plot twist instead of writing | Write 50 rough words on my current draft. |
| Researching another idea online | Close the browser and journal one actionable step. |
| Planning future scenes in my head | Set a 10-minute timer and draft one quick bullet. |
| Daydreaming about book launch success | Write one sentence of character dialogue. |
| Creating character art instead of story | Freewrite for 5 minutes about today's scene. |
| Tweaking worldbuilding details endlessly | Outline the next two paragraphs in my story. |

**JOURNAL PROMPT**

When do your daydream detours shows up most in your writing process? Is it when you're first drafting, outlining details, polishing a scene, or other?

# shift your writing mindset

**Your imagination is a gift . . . until it becomes a detour.**

When you're a Dreamer, your mindset is often focused on the possibilities swirling in your head. But that mindset keeps you dawdling in daydreams instead of landing on the page. Changing your mindset doesn't mean abandoning your imagination—it means retraining your inner voice to value small steps so you can move forward.

## MINDSET REFRAME #1

**Old mindset:** "I need more inspiration before I start."
**New mindset:** "Ideas come to life when I take action."
Daydreams feel safe, but they keep you from discovering what your ideas truly need. Imagining the perfect moment or the perfect scene might feel inspiring, but only experimenting on the page will reveal what actually works. You don't have to have every detail in place before you begin; just try one small piece and let your imagination evolve through doing.

**Reflect:**
When was the last time you waited for "inspiration" and it never arrived?

_____

What's one tiny experiment you could do today, just to see where your idea might lead when you take the first step?

_____

## MINDSET REFRAME #2

**Old mindset:** "I need the perfect idea before I write a single word."
**New mindset:** "Writing reveals the perfect idea."
Waiting for your "best" concept can trap you in idea-roulette. True discovery happens on the page when you explore, experiment, and refine. Instead of feeling like your masterpiece must be fully formed in your head before you start, simply start to coax it out.
**Reflect:**
What story fragment or character moment have you hesitated to try "because it wasn't fully baked"?

_____

What's one imperfect sentence you could write right now to discover what comes next?

_____

**QUICK ACTION**

List two simple ways you'll remind yourself to move from dreaming into doing this week (i.e., sticky notes, audio alerts, phone alarms, other):

_____

_____

# your personal mindset reframe

Cultivating a new mindset as a Dreamer means honoring your creativity while keeping it grounded in action. Your reframe card will remind you to transform big ideas into small experiments so you can learn by doing, not just by imagining.

## STEP 1: RECOGNIZE THE PATTERN

What is a common thought you have that leads you to drift into daydreaming instead of writing? (Example: "I don't have the perfect idea yet.")

_____

_____

## STEP 2: WRITE A MORE GROUNDING PROMPT

What new prompt will you practice this week to turn your ideas into action?
(Example: "I'll write one sentence about my idea and see where it takes me.")

_____

_____

**MY INSPIRATION CARD**

Use an index card, sticky note, or whatever you like. Write it big, decorate it, or make a small "badge" for your writing space.

**Old thought I'm replacing:** _____

**New thought I'm practicing:** _____

# my hidden rewards

**Daydreaming feels inspiring, but it can leave you stuck in fantasy.**

Procrastination for Dreamers often means staying in the realm of big ideas rather than doing the small tasks that brings them to life. That rich imagination can deliver real payoffs: excitement, novelty, and an escape from the tedium of drafting. Yet those rewards come at a hidden cost: unfinished projects, stalled confidence, and the gap between vision and reality. By naming the true payoffs you get from putting work off, you build the self-awareness that sparks lasting change.

## WHAT ARE YOUR HIDDEN REWARDS?

**When I avoid my writing, I might be getting:** (check all that apply)

☐ A thrill of new possibilities without any follow-through.

☐ Creative variety so I never have to stick with one project.

☐ Freedom from the pressure to produce polished work.

☐ An easy hit of inspiration instead of the hard work of editing.

☐ A boost of confidence in my vision, even if it never materializes.

☐ Relief from the "boring" parts of writing, like research, structure, and revision.

☐ The comfort of a perfect mental draft I can imagine but never finish.

Other hidden payoffs I've noticed:

_____

_____

_____

_____

**JOURNAL PROMPT**

What have these hidden rewards cost you creatively, emotionally, and in your writing goals?

# future payoffs

Now imagine what happens when you bring even one dream into action. Which of these outcomes excite you most? (Check all that apply.)

**If I face the discomfort and show up anyway, I could gain:**

☐ Progress on a project that once lived only in my head.
☐ A habit of finishing scenes and chapters, not just imagining them.
☐ Confidence that my imagination has the discipline to pay off.
☐ The satisfaction of seeing my stories take shape on the page.
☐ A clearer bridge from wild ideas to crafted drafts.
☐ A stronger sense of creative momentum, not just inspiration.
☐ Pride in completed work that readers can experience.

## OTHER BENEFITS I WANT TO CLAIM

_____     _____

_____     _____

## DESIGN YOUR "DREAM TO DRAFT" CARD

As a Dreamer, it's easy to live in possibility without creating anything tangible. A visual reminder of your deeper "why" can ground your imagination in action. In the space below, write or sketch your own "Dream to Draft" Card. Use bullet points, quotes, or a mini-roadmap. Decorate it however you like, and keep it somewhere you'll see whenever you feel tempted to stay in brainstorm mode.

MY DREAM-TO-DRAFT CARD

# your new writer identity

## Instead of new ideas, what you need is follow-through.

Overcoming Dreamer-style procrastination isn't just about trying to gain more focus. It helps to go further and think about actually changing your identity to someone who implements their ideas. When you move from "I'm a writer who chases ideas" to "I'm a writer who brings ideas to life," you're not just building a new habit, but rewiring your self-image. Once you start seeing yourself as someone who follows through, your actions will naturally follow.

## MY WRITING IDENTITY SHIFT

### Step 1: How do you see yourself now?

Be honest: What stories do you tell yourself when you get stuck?  Here are common Dreamer identity thoughts:

- "I'm someone who lives in possibility but never lands."
- "I get lost in new ideas before finishing the last one."
- "I brainstorm endlessly but don't like drafting my stories."
- "I jump to a new project as soon as the first feels stale."

Now, write 3 beliefs, labels, or self-messages you often carry about yourself as a writer.

_____

_____

_____

### Step 2: Who do you want to become?

Imagine yourself six months from now. You're following through on your ideas, one at a time. What new self-messages would you love to carry? Examples:

- "I'm a writer who finishes what I start."
- "I turn one idea into a complete scene before seeking the next."
- "I trust the magic of the draft, not just the flash of inspiration."
- "I build momentum by completing small sections."

Write 3 beliefs you want to grow into.

_____

_____

_____

**Step 3: What would that version of you do next?**

Next, using the ideas you wrote down, create a simple statement that captures who you are becoming as a writer.

Try this formula:
**Even though I usually _____, I'm learning to _____.**

Here are some examples:
- Even though I usually abandon drafts at the first sign of boredom, I'm learning to finish one scene before starting another.
- Even though I usually chase the next big idea, I'm learning to take the steps that will bring that one idea to fruition first.
- Even though I usually wait for inspiration to strike again, I'm learning to write something every day.

## MY IDENTITY BRIDGE STATEMENT

_____

_____

_____

## ENCOURAGE YOURSELF!

**Remember:** Every small choice you make to finish a paragraph, complete a scene, or press "save" is a vote for the writer you're becoming. You can keep on dreaming as long as you practice finishing. This is your day to start acting like a writer who finishes.

> # *Though I love to brainstorm, I'm learning to focus on one idea long enough to bring it to life.*

# tools to bring your ideas to life

**Rather than endless daydreaming, use tools to keep your words flowing.**

As a Dreamer, your mind buzzes with possibilities, but too many ideas can leave you frozen in "what if" land. The tools in this section are like well-placed stepping stones: they guide you from idea into action, one small move at a time.

You don't have to sprint through every possibility at once. Pick one tool, test it, and watch your draft grow. Small progress creates momentum, and momentum brings you back to the page. With the right support, even the wildest vision can materialize.

## TOOLKIT FOR THE DREAMER

### Idea Parking Lot

When a new idea distracts you, jot it into an "Idea Parking Lot" (a notebook or doc) and return to your current scene. This honors your creativity without derailing progress.

### Single-Scene Sprint

Set a 20-minute timer and write one complete scene—beginning, middle, and end—before anything else. Lock in that momentum and resist chasing the next shiny thought.

### Limit Your List

If planning feels safer than drafting, restrict yourself to three bullet-point plot markers. No more. Then dive into the first one.

### Freewrite Flash

Give yourself 5 minutes of pure, unfiltered writing on your chosen scene. No editing, no second-guessing. Let the story speak.

### Visual Inspiration Ritual

Before writing, look at a photo or piece artwork that captures your current project's tone. Then write for 10 minutes inspired by that mood.

### Finish One Thing

Challenge yourself to finish one short piece, no matter how small. Could be a scene, paragraph, or sentence. Claim that win before you explore another idea.

### Draft-First, Edit Later

When you start questioning your idea, remind yourself: "This is a messy first draft, not the final cut." Write through imperfection and refine afterward.

### Your Turn!

## CHOOSE TWO TOOLS

After reviewing the toolkit, pick two strategies that feel most helpful for you right now. For each one, write a small, clear action step you'll take to practice this week.

*Examples:*
- If you choose Idea **Parking Lot** tool, your action step might be: "Tonight, I'll create a new document titled 'Idea Parking Lot' and transfer three half-written ideas into it before writing scene one."
- If you choose **Single-Scene Sprint** tool, your action step might be: "Tomorrow morning, I'll set a 20-minute timer and write the opening scene start to finish."
- If you choose **Visual Inspiration Ritual** tool, your action step might be: "Before writing tonight, I'll select one painting or photo that reflects my novel's mood, stare at it for two minutes, then write for 10 minutes."

## MY TOOLS AND ACTION STEPS

Tool #1 I'm Choosing:

_____

Action Step I'll Take:

_____

Tool #2 I'm Choosing:

_____

Action Step I'll Take:

_____

## THE DREAMER'S LAUNCH CUE

Dreamers have plenty of ideas. What they need is a trigger to launch into action. Write a brief cue—a word or phrase—that propels you from inspiration into writing. Examples:

- "One page at a time."
- "Finish before you chase."
- "Turn spark into paragraph."

**My personal cue:**

_____

# mapping your novel journey

**Take action for 7 days, even if it's just for five minutes.**

As a Dreamer, it's all too easy to float among ideas without landing on paper. Small, concrete actions help you bridge the gap from imagination to creation. Each tiny step you take builds the habit of following through, and before you know it, your ideas start becoming real stories.

## QUICK IDEAS FOR SMALL STEPS

(Choose or modify!)

- Sketch one paragraph of dialogue between two characters.
- Draft 100 words of an upcoming scene—no need for polish.
- Turn one of your brainstormed ideas into a bullet-point outline.
- Freewrite for five minutes on the "what if" that excites you most.
- Write a logline or Twitter pitch for your story in 280 characters or less.
- Post a one-sentence teaser about your project in your writing group.
- Spend 10 minutes mapping your story's next turning point.

## MY SMALL STEPS FOR THE WEEK

| Day | One small action... | Did I take it? |
|---|---|---|
| Monday | | |
| Tuesday | | |
| Wednesday | | |
| Thursday | | |
| Friday | | |
| Saturday | | |
| Sunday | | |

## NOVEL-WRITING ROADMAP

### Step 1: Pick Your Spark

- Identify one vivid moment or image in your story world.
- Write 100 words describing that moment. Have fun! It doesn't have to be perfect.
- Embrace that spark as your creative fuel, not your final product.

*Example:*
- "I'll write about the moment my hero first sees the glowing portal."
- "I'll describe the sound and smell of rain in my fantasy city."

**My spark:**

_____

### Step 2: Turn Ideas into Tiny Outlines

- Write one-sentence loglines for three key scenes you're most excited about.
- Jot down 3-5 bullet points for each logline to sketch the scene's beats.
- Keep it loose—no more than 10 minutes per scene.

*Example:*
- Logline: "A runaway princess hides in the streets and befriends a street musician." Beats: Princess flees palace • hides in tavern • meets musician • calms her fear.

**My tiny outlines:**

_____

### Step 3: Capture Creative Momentum

- Schedule three brief "idea-to-page" sessions per week (10-20 minutes).
- After each session, jot one line about what surprised you.
- Use a creative trigger like your favorite music or a scented candle to signal "play."

*Examples:*
- Monday morning: 10 minutes freewrite with jazz playing.
- Wednesday afternoon: sketch a character and write one sentence about them.
- Friday evening: light a candle, read your favorite prompt, then draft 50 words.

**My momentum boost:**

_____

# carry your action forward

**When you focus your spark, the writing begins to glow.**

As a Dreamer, your gift is a kaleidoscope of possibilities. Just remember that the real magic happens when you ignite that one spark on the page. Indulge your imagination, but then choose one flash of inspiration to catch and let it guide your next move. Below are common Dreamer thoughts and playful reframes to turn your bursts of vision into writing action.

## SHIFT YOUR SELF-TALK

| Dreamer Thought | Action Reframe |
|---|---|
| "I have too many ideas." | "Focusing on one idea helps me discover its hidden possibilities." |
| "I get bored when actually writing." | "Even a few sentences can spark new excitement." |
| "What if this isn't the best choice?" | "Every choice teaches me something I can use later." |
| "I never finish." | "I can complete one project before adding the next." |

**Your Turn**

Write down a Dreamer thought and answer with a new action-oriented voice.

| Dreamer Thought | Action Reframe |
|---|---|
|  |  |
|  |  |
|  |  |
|  |  |

## YOUR ACTION PLAN

**1. What's one action-focused reminder I can use when tempted to daydream?**
(Example: "Pick one idea and write one paragraph.")

_____

**2. What's one grounding ritual I can use to shift quickly from ideas to writing?**
(Example: Opening a specific writing file; setting a short timer.)

_____

**3. What's one satisfying way I'll celebrate finishing each small writing step?**
(Example: Checking off a writing tracker, posting "I wrote!" in my writing group.)

_____

## LOOKING BACK

Every time you swap a "too many ideas" loop for a "just one step" prompt, you remind yourself that creativity grows through doing. Old habits like endless brainstorming, idea overload, and waiting for inspiration may still mess you up sometimes. But now you've built new strengths:

- Awareness of your dreaming tendencies.
- Tools to guide your flights of fancy into form.
- A writer identity rooted in _action_.
- Proof that dreaming plus doing equals discovery.

## action commitment

> # I commit to turning one idea into action each day—one spark at a time.

Signed: _____

Date: _____

# meet the fun-seeker

**You procrastinate when writing starts to feel boring, hard, or repetitive.**

You want to write, but the spark has to be there. If the scene feels slow or the structure too rigid, you lose interest. You tell yourself you'll come back to it later, when you're more inspired. But as a Fun Seeker, your procrastination often shows up as avoidance of anything that doesn't feel exciting or new.

You might jump from project to project, get distracted by social media, or spend your writing time chasing more stimulating activities. You love writing, but sustained focus can feel stifling, and your creativity craves novelty.

The problem? Fun-seeking becomes your default escape route when writing gets tough. And while spontaneity is part of your gift, too much of it keeps you from finishing what matters most. In this section, you'll learn how to recognize your patterns and tap into creative momentum, even when things aren't thrilling.

## COMMON TRAITS OF A FUN-SEEKER WRITER

- Struggle to stick with a project once the excitement wears off.
- Get bored during slower phases like outlining, revising, or editing.
- Abandon current work for a newer, shinier idea.
- Find writing structure or discipline stifling.
- Procrastinate by scrolling, snacking, or jumping to other hobbies.
- Feel restless when writing feels repetitive or "too serious."
- Have dozens of half-finished drafts you rarely return to.

## SELF-CHECK: DO YOU RECOGNIZE THIS PATTERN?

Check all that apply:
- ☐ I get excited about new ideas but quickly lose steam.
- ☐ I avoid writing sessions that feel slow, confusing, or repetitive.
- ☐ I often tell myself I'll come back to a project later—but I don't.
- ☐ I procrastinate when the writing requires sustained focus.
- ☐ I use fun distractions to escape from writing tasks I find dull.
- ☐ I get bored with structure or routine, even when it helps me.
- ☐ I struggle to finish what I start, even when I still love the idea.

# fun-channeling matrix

When your mind starts whispering that it's time for something more enjoyable, or when distraction threatens your momentum, use the fun-channeling matrix below. Quickly identify your procrastination trigger, then immediately engage in the small paired action to recapture your attention and spark creative enjoyment again.

| When I catch myself... | Then I will... |
|---|---|
| **Thinking, "This is getting boring . . ."** | Set a 10-minute creative timer to make it fun. |
| **Feeling tempted by social media or games** | Write one paragraph as if my character played it. |
| **Considering abandoning my current project** | Outline one surprising twist to re-engage myself. |
| **Feeling stuck or uninspired** | Change my writing location or put on fun music. |
| **Avoiding routine tasks like editing or revising** | Make it into a playful game with rewards. |
| **Noticing I've lost excitement** | Switch briefly to a playful brainstorming exercise. |
| **Feeling the urge to pursue something new.** | Quickly note the new idea, then return to task. |

**JOURNAL PROMPT**

Where in your writing routine do you most often feel tempted to seek fun elsewhere? Is it drafting, editing, marketing, or something else entirely?

# shift your writing mindset

**Fun can be created, not just found.**

As a Fun Seeker, your mindset is often centered on avoiding anything that feels dull, repetitive, or confining. You might think, "If this isn't fun, I shouldn't be doing it." But waiting for inspiration or jumping to the next shiny idea often leaves your stories half-finished and your confidence shaky. Changing your mindset means retraining your inner voice to find small sparks of fun in the process of showing up, staying curious, and finishing what you started.

## MINDSET REFRAME #1

**Old mindset:** "If it's not exciting, I can't write."
**New mindset:** "I can make the writing fun again."
It's easy to assume that excitement should come first, but often, it's the act of writing that reignites the spark. You can create momentum by bringing playfulness to the page through curiosity, small creative risks, or writing rituals that make you smile.

**Reflect:**
When was the last time you abandoned a project just because it lost its thrill?

_____

What's one way you could add fun back into that project, even just for today?

_____

## MINDSET REFRAME #2

**Old mindset:** "If I'm not inspired, it won't be good."
**New mindset:** "Inspiration grows when I engage."
By showing up consistently and experimenting even when you're not "feeling it," you train your creative brain to respond. Boredom isn't a sign of failure. It's often a doorway into something deeper and more surprising.

**Reflect:**
Think of a time when you started writing without much inspiration. What happened once you got into it?

_____

What's one project you can return to this week, just to see where it takes you?

_____

## QUICK ACTION

List two ways you'll remind yourself of these new mindsets during your writing sessions (i.e., a colorful sticky note, a playlist called "Just Start," a five-minute "play first" timer):

_____

_____

# your personal mindset reframe

Changing your mindset means choosing a message that helps you show up with joy, even when the fun fades. In the space below, create your own personalized reframe that speaks directly to how your Fun Seeker brain tries to drift and how your focused creative self will bring you back.

## STEP 1: RECOGNIZE THE PATTERN

What's a common thought or excuse you use to skip writing when it stops feeling exciting? (Example: "This part's boring. I'll write later.")

_____

_____

## STEP 2: WRITE A MORE ENCOURAGING TRUTH

What's a playful or grounded message you'll practice this week to keep going anyway? (Example: "Even boring scenes have magic once I get into them.")

_____

_____

### MY MAKE-IT-FUN CARD

Use an index card, sticky note, or whatever you like. Write it big, decorate it, or make a small "badge" for your writing space.

**Old thought I'm replacing:** _____

**New thought I'm practicing:** _____

# my hidden rewards

**Chasing excitement feels energizing, but it steals the joy of finishing.**

For you, procrastination is a way to keep things interesting. Your brain naturally looks for stimulation, variety, and creative highs. So when writing slows down or starts to feel routine, your mind says: "Let's do something more exciting." That detour may feel good in the moment, but it often keeps you from the long-term satisfaction of completing the stories you care about. By getting honest about the real rewards your brain is chasing and the deeper payoffs you truly want, you can start shifting toward meaningful fun, not just fleeting escape.

## WHAT ARE YOUR HIDDEN REWARDS?

**When I avoid my writing, I might be getting:** (check all that apply)

☐ A hit of instant gratification from something more stimulating.

☐ Relief from tasks that feel repetitive or "boring."

☐ A sense of freedom by avoiding structure or deadlines.

☐ The thrill of chasing a new idea instead of finishing the old one.

☐ A break from writing tasks that feel too slow or technical.

☐ Temporary pleasure from switching to something easier.

☐ A way to avoid committing in case it stops being fun.

Other hidden payoffs I've noticed:

_____

_____

_____

_____

**JOURNAL PROMPT**

What have these short-term rewards been costing you, creatively, emotionally, or in your writing dreams? Have they helped you, or are they starting to hold you back?

# future payoffs

Now imagine the rewards you'll unlock by sticking with your writing, even when it's not instantly exciting. Which of these outcomes spark your energy or motivation? (Check all that apply.)

**If I face the discomfort and show up anyway, I could gain:**

☐ The thrill of finishing something I actually care about.
☐ A deeper sense of creative flow and focus.
☐ Proof that I can follow through, not just start strong.
☐ A writing rhythm that feels engaging and sustainable.
☐ Confidence in my ability to stick with a story through the boring parts.
☐ New inspiration that comes from seeing things through.
☐ A sense of purpose that outlasts momentary excitement.

## OTHER BENEFITS I WANT TO CLAIM

_____     _____

_____     _____

## DESIGN YOUR "IGNITE-AND-GO!" CARD

Your Ignite-and-Go! card is a fast, fun way to reconnect with your excitement and move it into action. Use it anytime your motivation dips or your brain starts chasing something shinier. In the space below, use phrases, bullets, doodles, quotes, or a short mantra to capture what excites you about writing, and how you'll keep it playful when things slow down. Decorate it later if you want, and post it where it'll spark action.

MY IGNITE-AND-GO! CARD

# your new writer identity

**Instead of seeking more inspiration, find a rhythm that keeps you moving.**

Overcoming procrastination involves changing what you do, but also changing how you see yourself. When you shift from "I'm a writer who gets bored and bails" to "I'm a writer who brings the fun and follows through," you're building new habits while simultaneously stepping into a new identity. Once you believe in your ability to keep going—even when the thrill wears off—everything else gets easier.

## MY WRITING IDENTITY SHIFT

### Step 1: How do you see yourself now?

Let's be honest about how you tend to view yourself as a writer, especially when things get slow or hard. Here are common Fun-Seeker identity thoughts:

- "I'm someone who always starts strong but loses steam."
- "I write best when I'm inspired, so I wait for inspiration."
- "I jump to a new idea whenever this one gets boring."
- "I can't stay focused long enough to finish anything."

Now, write 3 beliefs, labels, or self-messages you often carry about yourself as a writer.

_____

_____

_____

### Step 2: Who do you want to become?

Imagine it's six months from now. You've been showing up, finishing things, and finding fun in the process. What would your self-talk sound like then? Examples:

- "I'm a writer who creates my own momentum."
- "I stick with projects because they matter to me."
- "I know how to make writing fun, even when it's not thrilling."
- "I finish what I start and that feels amazing!"

Write 3 beliefs you want to grow into.

_____

_____

_____

**Step 3: What would that version of you do next?**
Next, using the ideas you wrote down, create a simple statement that captures who you are becoming as a writer.

Try this formula:
**Even though I usually _____, I'm learning to _____.**

Here are some examples:

- Even though I usually quit when I lose interest, I'm learning to follow through anyway.
- Even though I usually chase new ideas, I'm learning to finish what I start.
- Even though I usually wait to feel excited, I'm learning to write to create excitement.

## MY IDENTITY BRIDGE STATEMENT

_____

_____

_____

## ENCOURAGE YOURSELF!

**Remember:** Every time you choose to stay with your work even after the buzz fades or the fun dips, you're showing yourself something powerful: You're a writer who knows how to make your work fun along the way. By doing so, you become a writer who hangs in there—a writer who finishes their projects.

> *I may still get bored from time to time, but I'm learning to stay and make it fun!*

# tools to follow through

**Your energy is a gift, but without direction, it fizzles before it finishes.**

You love fresh ideas, fast starts, and the thrill of discovery. But when the fun fades, your instinct is to bail. Just telling yourself to do better, though, probably won't work. It will only set you up for failure.

You need tools that help you channel your creative energy. Think of them like a skatepark: boundaries that make your wild ideas work. These tools help you stay in motion when motivation dips so you can carry your momentum forward all the way to "done."

## TOOLKIT FOR THE FUN-SEEKER

### Try a Writing Sprint Game

Set a timer for 10 minutes and challenge yourself to write without stopping. Bonus points if you can beat your word count the next round.

### Switch Up the Format

Write a scene in list form, dialogue only, or as a text thread just to get it done in a fun way.

### Add a Surprise to Your Scene

Feeling bored? Throw in a twist. A surprise character, an unexpected emotion, a new obstacle. Keep it fresh to keep going.

### Use a "Finish Line" Countdown

Make a mini challenge: "Three more paragraphs and I get a dance break." Count backward from 5 tasks left, not up from 0.

### Change the Environment

Write from a coffee shop, on the floor, in your car, or any place that sparks energy without derailing focus.

### Reward Every Session

Build in mini-rewards for completing even 10 minutes. Try a sticker, song, silly dance, treat, dinner out, walk in the park, or social share.

### Create a "Bored but Writing" Playlist

Pick music that makes you feel alive even when your brain wants to wander. Use it only when writing to spark good energy.

### Your Turn!

## CHOOSE TWO TOOLS

After reviewing the toolkit, pick two strategies that feel most helpful for you right now. For each one, write a small, clear action step you'll take to practice this week.

*Examples:*
- If you choose **Writing Sprint Game,** your action step might be: "Do one 10-minute sprint tomorrow and count the words."
- If you choose **Finish Line Countdown,** your action step might be: "Break my task into 5 micro steps and check off each one."
- If you choose **Reward Every Session**, your action step might be: "Give myself a sticker after every 15-minute writing block."

## MY TOOLS AND ACTION STEPS

Tool #1 I'm Choosing:

_____

Action Step I'll Take:

_____

Tool #2 I'm Choosing:

_____

Action Step I'll Take:

_____

## THE FUN-SEEKER'S FINISH PHRASE

Fun Seekers don't struggle with starting, they struggle with staying. What you need in that moment is a spark of playful direction; a phrase that pulls you back into momentum without killing your vibe.

- "One more scene, then dance."
- "The finish line is the fun."
- "Momentum is a better thrill."

**My finish phrase:**

_____

# mapping your novel journey

**Turn little actions into lasting momentum. You can make each one fun!**

The creative path isn't always thrilling. When your writing starts to feel slow or repetitive, it's easy to drift away. Tiny, focused actions keep the spark alive. Remember that *you* are the one responsible for injecting fun into your writing process. You don't have to do a ton of work—just little steps that build momentum.

## QUICK IDEAS FOR SMALL STEPS

(Choose or modify!)

- Write a short scene you've actually been daydreaming about.
- Open your draft and bold your favorite line.
- Add one surprising detail to your current scene.
- Make a list of weird, funny, or chaotic plot twists.
- Rewrite one paragraph in a totally different tone just for fun.
- Give your character a secret and journal about it.
- Start a "line dump" page and write five random bits of dialogue.

## MY SMALL STEPS FOR THE WEEK

| Day | One small action... | Did I take it? |
|---|---|---|
| Monday | | |
| Tuesday | | |
| Wednesday | | |
| Thursday | | |
| Friday | | |
| Saturday | | |
| Sunday | | |

## NOVEL-WRITING ROADMAP

### Step 1: Make It Fun to Begin

- Jump into the part of the story you're most excited about.
- Set a "low-pressure" session goal like: "Write something weird for 15 minutes."
- Use prompts, music, or visuals to kickstart your curiosity.

*Examples:*
- "I'll write the confrontation scene. It sounds fun."
- "I'll scribble five lines of banter between my favorite characters."

**My fun start:**

---

### Step 2: Outline in Playful Layers

- Write a one-sentence "movie trailer" version of your story.
- Create a five-point "roadmap" of major beats—no pressure to follow it exactly.
- Use sticky notes or index cards for a mix-and-match scene list.

*Examples:*
- "Rebel enters town • crush appears • big lie is exposed • betrayal • revenge"
- Scene cards: First kiss → Major setback → Plot twist → Funny fail → Final showdown

**My layered outlines:**

---

### Step 3: Make Finishing a Game

- Choose two short writing sessions a week. Make them themed ("Wild Draft Wednesday").
- Track your effort with a color chart, sticker, or song playlist.
- Pair writing with a reward: fun snack, walk, or 10 minutes of YouTube.

*Examples:*
- On Tuesdays, I write 200 wild words before breakfast and blast a power anthem.
- Each Friday, I write for 20 minutes and then binge one YouTube video guilt-free.

**My game boost:**

---

# carry your spark forward

**When you direct your spark, you fuel real momentum.**

Finishing something meaningful often requires coming back to the page even when the initial excitement fades. With a few focus-friendly habits and a deeper sense of purpose, you can keep your momentum alive and see your projects through with joy and satisfaction. Below are common thoughts that pull Fun Seekers off track along with some tips that help you shift them into focus-friendly reframes.

## SHIFT YOUR SELF-TALK

| Fun-Seeker Thought | Spark Reframe |
|---|---|
| "This is getting boring." | "Boring is just a sign I'm building momentum." |
| "I'll come back to this later." | "Ten more minutes now means real progress." |
| "I need something more exciting." | "I can make this scene more fun, or power through and play after." |
| "I'll just start something new." | "I'll finish this moment, then I'll try something fresh." |

### Your Turn

Write down a Fun-Seeker thought and answer with a new spark-oriented voice.

| Fun-Seeker Thought | Spark Reframe |
|---|---|
|  |  |
|  |  |
|  |  |
|  |  |

## YOUR SPARK-IT PLAN

**1. What's one action-focused reminder I can use when tempted to daydream?**
(Example: "Pick one idea and write one paragraph.")

_____

**2. What's one energizing ritual I can use to re-engage my focus before writing?**
(Examples: 3-minute playlist, micro dance break, drawing a card with a surprise prompt.)

_____

**3. How will I reward myself for sticking with the work, especially when it gets dull?**
(Examples: add a sticker to your finish tracker, watch a fav show, post a progress update.)

_____

## LOOKING BACK

Some writing days feel electric. Others... not so much. The real win? Showing up anyway. Each time you stick with your draft when your mind itches for something new, you're proving to yourself that you can stay connected to what matters. The old pattern will still tug at you sometimes. But you've got new tools now:

- Awareness of what throws you off.
- A writer identity that knows how to stay engaged.
- Quick-start strategies for when things get stale.
- Proof that you can bring your ideas to the finish line.

# spark commitment

*I commit to finishing the work that matters by showing up, staying with it, and finding fun in the follow-through.*

Signed: _____

Date: _____

# meet the perfectionist

**Your standards aren't just high . . . they're armor.**

You care deeply about your writing. Maybe too deeply at times. You want your words to be beautiful, your plot watertight, your character arcs emotionally satisfying, and your writing life to unfold with grace, discipline, and polish.

You likely hold yourself to high standards in other areas of life, too. You show up prepared, capable, and composed. You value meaning, mastery, and making something that truly matters. But underneath that drive is a more tender truth: you're afraid that if your work isn't perfect, it won't be good enough, and by extension, maybe you won't be either. So you fix. You polish. You delay sharing, scrap promising drafts, or spend all day editing one paragraph.

This section will help you spot when your pursuit of excellence is tipping into avoidance, and give you tools to reclaim the messy, powerful joy of creating.

## COMMON TRAITS OF A PERFECTIONIST WRITER

- Feel like your writing has to be flawless before anyone sees it.
- Spend more time editing than drafting.
- Struggle to finish anything because it never feels "done enough."
- Procrastinate starting because you're not sure it will turn out "right."
- Overresearch or outline endlessly instead of writing.
- Abandon projects when they fall short of your original vision.
- Fixate on external validation or fear harsh feedback.

## SELF-CHECK: DO YOU RECOGNIZE THIS PATTERN?

Check all that apply:
- ☐ I edit as I go and lose momentum.
- ☐ I restart the same project over and over, trying to "get it right."
- ☐ I compare my drafts to published books and feel discouraged.
- ☐ I obsess over sentence structure instead of telling the story.
- ☐ I work for hours and still feel it's not enough.
- ☐ I put off writing until I'm "in the zone."
- ☐ I avoid feedback unless I think something is *really* good.

# perfectionist's disruption matrix

Whenever your inner Perfectionist tightens its grip, come back to this matrix. Scan down the rows and across the columns for the pattern that best matches your stuck moment, then immediately do the paired micro-action. Every imperfect action teaches your brain that progress—not flawlessness—is the true path forward.

| When I catch myself... | Then I will... |
|---|---|
| Rewriting the same paragraph again | Write the *next* paragraph without looking back. |
| Avoiding drafting until it's perfect | Draft a messy version in 10 minutes, just to explore. |
| Polishing instead of progressing | Add 100 new words before editing anything. |
| Freezing on the first line | Write the second line first. |
| Obsessing over sentence rhythm | Tell the story like a friend would—fast and loose. |
| Starting over for the fifth time | Keep going past the messy part. Don't hit delete. |
| Refusing to share | Send it to a trusted reader for positive feedback. |

**JOURNAL PROMPT**

Where does your perfectionism slow you down the most? Starting a draft? Finishing it? Letting it be seen? What's one moment where your high standards get in the way of actual words on the page?

# shift your writing mindset

**Perfection may look like discipline, but it often disguises fear.**

You might think, "If I can make this flawless, I'll finally feel good about it." But perfectionism doesn't lead to confidence. Instead, it often blocks it. The more pressure you put on your work to be extraordinary, the harder it becomes to finish anything at all. Shifting your mindset changes the role perfection plays in your process. Instead of chasing flawlessness, you'll start valuing momentum, discovery, and creative growth. Progress builds confidence faster than polishing ever will.

## MINDSET REFRAME #1

**Old mindset:** "If it's not great, it's not worth writing."
**New mindset:** "Every messy draft teaches me how to make it better."
By demanding greatness up front, you protect yourself from the vulnerability of being seen in process. But here's the truth: Every finished book you love once started as a messy, flawed draft. When you let yourself show up imperfectly, you open the door to discovery.

**Reflect:**
When was the last time you stopped writing because it didn't meet your standards?

_____

What's one thing you could finish this week, just to practice showing up, even if it's messy?

_____

## MINDSET REFRAME #2

**Old mindset:** "I need to fix every flaw before moving forward."
**New mindset:** "Done is better than perfect, because done teaches me what works."
Constant editing keeps you in one place—trapped in chapter one or circling the same paragraph for weeks. When you give yourself permission to move on, you build trust in your creative flow. You don't have to get it right today. You just have to keep going.

**Reflect:**
Where in your writing process do you tend to over-polish or endlessly revise?

_____

What's one step you can take this week without fixing anything first?

_____

**QUICK ACTION**

List two ways you'll keep these new mindsets visible during your writing week (i.e., sticky notes, daily reminders, a "permission to be messy" alarm):

_____

_____

# your personal mindset reframe

Changing your mindset is about choosing a message that keeps you moving even when your inner perfectionist protests. In the space below, create a reframe that speaks to your biggest perfectionist hang-up, and the wiser, braver option you'll practice instead.

## STEP 1: RECOGNIZE THE PATTERN

What is a common thought that derails your writing momentum?
(Example: "It has to be amazing or it's not worth doing.")

_____

_____

## STEP 2: WRITE A MORE ENCOURAGING TRUTH

What thought will help you keep writing, even if it's not perfect?
(Example: "My job is to draft, not to impress.")

_____

_____

 **MY INNER-PERMISSION CARD**

Use an index card, sticky note, or whatever you like. Write it big, decorate it, or make a small "badge" for your writing space.

**Old thought I'm replacing:** _____

**New thought I'm practicing:** _____

# my hidden rewards

### What's perfection giving you that keeps you trapped?

It's easy to confuse procrastination with "not working" at all, but for the Perfectionist, it often *is* work, because it involves tweaking, fixing, overthinking, and endlessly polishing. It feels productive, but it actually prevents forward motion. By identifying the real payoffs your brain is chasing when you procrastinate this way, you begin to loosen the grip of perfectionism. With that awareness, you can start choosing progress over pressure and momentum over fear.

## WHAT ARE YOUR HIDDEN REWARDS?

### When I avoid my writing, I might be getting: (check all that apply)

☐ A sense of control by endlessly refining.

☐ Relief from the anxiety of sharing imperfect work.

☐ Protection of my self-image as a "good" writer.

☐ Avoidance of the discomfort of not meeting my own high expectations.

☐ Escape from feelings of self-doubt, shame, or comparison.

☐ The illusion of "working" without taking risks.

☐ A reason not to finish so I don't have to be judged.

Other hidden payoffs I've noticed:

_____

_____

_____

_____

### JOURNAL PROMPT

What has the pursuit of perfection been costing you creatively, emotionally, or in terms of your writing progress?

# future payoffs

Now imagine what could change if you gave yourself permission to move forward even before your writing is perfect. Which of these outcomes feel meaningful to you? (Check all that apply.)

**If I release the need to get it perfect, I could gain:**

☐ A finished draft that I can shape, explore, and improve.
☐ Confidence from actually completing something.
☐ A deeper connection with readers through real, imperfect work.
☐ Clarity about my voice by experimenting more freely.
☐ Greater creative energy from letting things be "good enough."
☐ Relief from the exhausting cycle of endless tweaking.
☐ Trust in myself to handle imperfection and grow from it.

**OTHER BENEFITS I WANT TO CLAIM**

_____     _____

_____     _____


**DESIGN YOUR "LET-IT-BE-DONE" CARD**

When perfection creeps in, it whispers: *It's not ready. It's not right. Fix it again.* But done is a powerful act. Done teaches you more than waiting ever will. In the space below, create your own "Let-It-Be-Done" card—a personal reminder that forward motion matters more than flawlessness. Use bullet points, bold declarations, mantras, or visual elements. Make it something you can keep nearby as you write.

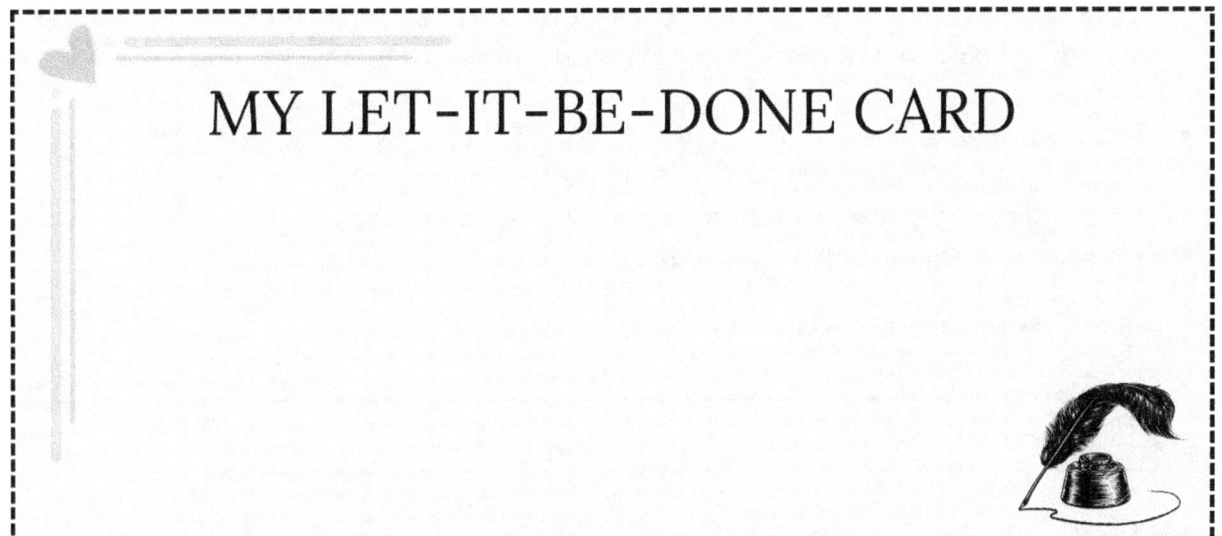

MY LET-IT-BE-DONE CARD

# your new writer identity

**Perfect pages don't build your writing life. Finished ones do.**

The "perfectionist" identity can feel like a badge of honor, but it often keeps you stuck in an endless loop of fixing, redoing, and never quite moving forward. To shift, you have to change how you see yourself. Instead as someone who gets it "right" or "flawless," how about someone who makes progress every day? You just have to start believing that imperfect progress still counts and that you're allowed to finish before you figure it all out.

## MY WRITING IDENTITY SHIFT

### Step 1: How do you see yourself now?

Let's get honest: What messages do you hear in your head when writing doesn't go "perfectly"? Here are some common Perfectionist identity thoughts:

- "I'm someone who can't stop until it's just right."
- "I don't count as a writer unless my work is excellent."
- "I revise so much that I never make real progress."
- "I freeze if I can't match the vision in my head."

Now, write 3 beliefs, labels, or self-messages you often carry about yourself as a writer.

_____

_____

_____

### Step 2: Who do you want to become?

Now picture yourself six months from now. You're more relaxed, productive, and willing to create without judgment. What self-messages do you want to hold instead? Examples:

- "I'm a writer who finishes things, even when they're messy."
- "I treat progress as more important than perfection."
- "I write bravely without waiting for everything to be polished."
- "I'm someone who explores first drafts and trusts the process."

Write 3 beliefs you want to grow into.

_____

_____

_____

**Step 3: What would that version of you do next?**
Next, using the ideas you wrote down, create a simple statement that captures who you are becoming as a writer.

Try this formula:
**Even though I usually** _____, **I'm learning to** _____.

Here are some examples:

- Even though I usually edit the same sentence ten times, I'm learning to move forward and revise later.
- Even though I usually freeze if something isn't coming out right, I'm learning to keep going with curiosity.
- Even though I usually get stuck chasing "perfect," I'm learning to finish my ideas first.

## MY IDENTITY BRIDGE STATEMENT

_____

_____

_____

## ENCOURAGE YOURSELF!

**Remember:** Every time you keep going, even when the writing feels rough, you're building the muscle of completion. You're proving to yourself that done matters more than dazzling. Progress, not perfection, is how real writers grow.

> *I'm learning to value my work, no matter what. I'm learning to let it go and move on.*

# tools to set aside perfectionism

**Let your tools do the refining. Your job is to create.**

Perfectionism loves rules, precision, and polish. But it's progress, not polish, that finishes books. These tools aren't here to lower your standards, but to liberate you from the pressure to get everything right on the first try.

Think of them as creative levers: small, smart strategies that break the cycle of endless rewriting or editing and help you keep moving forward. Choose a few that feel doable and let them interrupt the spiral when your perfectionist brain kicks in.

## TOOLKIT FOR THE PERFECTIONIST

### Set a "Draft Ugly" Timer

Commit to writing without editing for 15 minutes. Use a prompt like "This draft isn't meant to impress anyone."

### Create a "Messy is Allowed" Space

Designate a document, notebook, or folder that's only for rough work. Nothing polished goes here—only raw, brave beginnings.

### Limit Revision Loops

Choose a number—say, two—and allow yourself only that many editing passes per paragraph before moving on.

### Use the 80% Rule

When you hit 80% satisfaction, stop. Remind yourself: Done and shared beats endlessly "improved" and hidden.

### Write to a Trusted Reader

Instead of trying to impress an invisible critic, write a draft like you're telling the story to a friend who gets you.

### Build a Post-Draft Reward

Pair writing with something joyful after the work is done. Not after it's perfect. After it's done!

### Use a Soft Startup

If you're frozen, begin by journaling about what's blocking you. Write about the writing until you're warmed up enough to begin.

### Your Turn!

## CHOOSE TWO TOOLS

After reviewing the toolkit, pick two strategies that feel most helpful for you right now. For each one, write a small, clear action step you'll take to practice it this week.

*Examples:*
- If you choose the **Draft Ugly Timer,** your step might be: "Set a timer for 15 minutes and draft without deleting anything."
- If you choose the **Messy is Allowed** space, your step might be: "Open a blank doc titled 'Draft Dump' and spill one messy page into it."
- If you choose **Post-Draft Reward,** your step might be: "Plan a cup of fancy tea after finishing a 300-word session."

## MY TOOLS AND ACTION STEPS

Tool #1 I'm Choosing:

_____

Action Step I'll Take:

_____

Tool #2 I'm Choosing:

_____

Action Step I'll Take:

_____

## THE PERFECTIONIST'S PERMISSION SLIP

This challenge invites you to create a phrase that welcomes imperfection while honoring your effort. Choose something short and strong enough to keep you writing when your inner critic sharpens its claws.

- "This doesn't have to be brilliant. It just has to exist on the page."
- "My words don't have to be flawless to be meaningful."
- There will always be something that's not perfect. It's okay to let it go.

**My permission slip:**

_____

# mapping your novel journey

**Consistency builds confidence, even if it's messy.**

Perfectionism tells you to wait until everything is just right. But that keeps you waiting and waiting, because nothing will ever be "just right." You can break out of this loop by taking baby steps. These small, imperfect actions help you stay connected to your writing without falling into endless revision cycles.

## QUICK IDEAS FOR SMALL STEPS

(Choose or modify!)

- Open your draft and highlight one paragraph you won't edit today.
- Freewrite for 5 minutes without deleting a single word.
- Write one scene in shorthand or summary form—no pressure for beauty.
- Add five bullet points to your outline (not perfect, just ideas).
- Pick one sentence and rewrite it three different ways just for fun.
- Journal what you're avoiding in your draft and why.
- Label one awkward paragraph or scene: "It's a placeholder, and that's okay for now."

## MY SMALL STEPS FOR THE WEEK

| Day | One small action... | Did I take it? |
|---|---|---|
| Monday | | |
| Tuesday | | |
| Wednesday | | |
| Thursday | | |
| Friday | | |
| Saturday | | |
| Sunday | | |

## NOVEL-WRITING ROADMAP

### Step 1: Make It Feel Safe to Start

- Begin with a low-stakes scene that sounds fun.
- Use a "placeholder" scene or sentence where you're stuck.
- Give yourself permission to write the worst version of a scene.

*Example:*
- "I'll write the dialogue first. I'll worry about setting later."
- "This scene scares me, so I'll just jot bullet points today."

**My safe start:**

_____

### Step 2: Outline with Breathing Room

- Write a one-sentence "movie trailer" version of your story.
- Create a five-point "roadmap" of major beats. No pressure to follow it exactly.
- Use sticky notes or index cards for a mix-and-match scene list.

*Example:*
- Hook • Big decision • Major setback • Turning point • Resolution
- Post-its: "Intro conflict," "Character blow-up," "Plot twist," "Resolution idea"

**My breathable outlines:**

_____

### Step 3: Write with Lower Stakes

- If your perfectionism is leading you to delay, choose 2 short writing sessions a week.
- Reward effort, not elegance.
- Allow awkward drafts, and set limits on how many editing drafts you'll allow.

*Examples:*
- "I'll write for 20 minutes and then stop. Quality doesn't matter at this point."
- "After writing, I'll journal what felt good instead of what felt 'off.'

**My lower-stakes boost:**

_____

# carry your permission forward

**Return to the page as a creator, not a judge.**

Perfectionism can easily become a cage. Creative writing, on the other hand, doesn't demand perfection, but only progress. It invites you to practice, grow, get feedback, improve, and keep going even when you feel uncertain. When you shift how you talk to yourself, especially when you're stuck, you begin to build a kinder, more sustainable writing life. Below, you'll practice that shift.

## SHIFT YOUR SELF-TALK

| Perfectionist Thought | Permission Reframe |
|---|---|
| **"This is already bad!"** | "This is version one. Every great draft starts rough." |
| **"I can't move on until this part is perfect."** | "I'm allowing only X drafts before this goes to my editor or beta reader." |
| **"This still isn't right. What's wrong with me?"** | "Writing is problem-solving. Every revision is a step forward." |
| **Nothing is ever good enough.** | "I'm getting better and better every day." |

**Your Turn**

Write down a Perfectionist thought and answer with a new permission-oriented voice.

| Perfectionist Thought | Permission Reframe |
|---|---|
|  |  |
|  |  |
|  |  |
|  |  |

## YOUR PERMISSION PLAN

**1. What's one thing I want to remind myself when perfectionism creeps in?**
(Example: "It's okay to write badly. Clarity comes later.")

_____

**2. What's one simple strategy or ritual I'll use to help me keep moving?**
(Examples: rough-draft timer, mantra, "no-backspace" session, five-minute warm-up.)

_____

**3. What's one way I'll reward myself for showing up—even when it's hard?**
(Examples: a favorite playlist, a sticker chart, 10 guilt-free minutes with a novel.)

_____

## LOOKING BACK

Each time you choose progress over perfection, you loosen the grip of procrastination. Your worth as a writer isn't measured by flawlessness, but shaped by your willingness to return and tap into the joy of creating. You have the tools now:

- Awareness of your perfectionist patterns.
- Tools to interrupt over-polishing.
- A more empowering writing identity.
- Evidence that you can move forward, even when it's not "perfect."

# permission commitment

*I give myself permission to write without perfection. Each page I create is proof that I'm growing and learning.*

Signed: _____

Date: _____

# meet the crisis-maker ⚠️

**You wait for the pressure to rise before you finally let yourself write.**

You have ideas. Ambitions. Even deadlines. But instead of starting, you squeeze in one more errand, one more scroll, one more "essential" task. Then, when the pressure hits, you explode into action! You pull the all-nighter. You race the clock. And sometimes you even win.

But the wins may not feel good for long. You may struggle to recover, experience burnout, or wonder why you keep repeating this pattern. As a Crisis-Maker, you like last-minute races. You're responsive, which is why pressure feels like a trigger. But you can't live (or write) in a constant state of chaos.

This section will help you learn how to generate urgency without self-destruction and build a steady pace that keeps your creative fire alive.

## COMMON TRAITS OF A CRISIS-MAKER WRITER

- Put off writing until a deadline or external pressure looms.
- Say "I work best under pressure," then keep proving it.
- Start a writing project way too late, then race to finish it.
- Feel driven during crunch time but lost when things are calm.
- Depend on last-minute adrenaline to spark motivation.
- Write in big, exhausting bursts that leave you drained.
- Feel resentful of the writing process even though you love it.

## SELF-CHECK: DO YOU RECOGNIZE THIS PATTERN?

Check all that apply:
- ☐ I often wait until the last possible minute to begin writing.
- ☐ I feel bored or distracted unless there's an urgent reason to write.
- ☐ I rely on caffeine, chaos, or a ticking clock to get started.
- ☐ I've pulled more than one all-nighter to finish writing.
- ☐ I write in unhealthy sprints that leave me creatively fried.
- ☐ I finish projects, but often at the cost of my well-being.
- ☐ I tell myself "I'll just wait until I have to" even when I don't want to.

# the pace-builder matrix

Whenever you notice your inner Crisis-Maker delaying until the last minute, pause and scan this matrix. Find the row that matches how you're currently stuck, and follow the action beside it right away. These small, proactive steps train your brain to create urgency on purpose so you don't always need a looming deadline to move.

| When I catch myself... | Then I will... |
| --- | --- |
| **Waiting for a deadline** | Set a pretend deadline and write for 20 minutes. |
| **Craving that "rush" feeling** | Use a countdown clock + upbeat playlist to create a mini-sprint. |
| **Doing everything except writing** | Choose one task to pause, and write one paragraph instead. |
| **Telling myself "I work better under pressure"** | Write 100 words before pressure hits; test the truth. |
| **Fantasizing about "writing all weekend"** | Schedule one 25-minute session today and show up. |
| **Feeling bored until panic starts** | Add novelty: switch location, style, or medium. |
| **Repeating "I'll start tomorrow"** | Start one sentence today, no matter how boring. |

**JOURNAL PROMPT**

When does the "I need pressure to perform" pattern show up most in your writing life? Is it tied to deadlines, boredom, fear of commitment, or something else? What do you think it costs you?

# shift your writing mindset

**You don't have to wait for pressure to perform. Small, steady effort can work.**

Deadlines, panic, and pressure tend to light a fire under you. Without that urgency, though, it's hard to get going. Part of you believes, "I only work well under pressure." But relying on crisis-mode takes a toll. It leads to burnout, missed opportunities, and a shaky sense of confidence. Shifting your mindset is about building a creative life that doesn't depend on panic. You'll learn to write with energy before the deadline looms and trust your consistency more than your stress.

## MINDSET REFRAME #1

**Old mindset:** "I need an immediate deadline to get anything done."
**New mindset:** "Steady effort builds stronger results."
Waiting for a time crunch to activate your creativity might work in the short term, but over time, it becomes a trap. Your brain begins to associate creativity with panic, not pleasure. Train yourself to work in short, energizing bursts before the deadline arrives.

**Reflect:**
When have you waited for urgency and then ended up overwhelmed?

_____

What's one low-pressure action you could take to prove you can start without a crisis?

_____

## MINDSET REFRAME #2

**Old mindset:** "I only do my best work when I'm under pressure."
**New mindset:** "My best work comes when I'm not burned out."
By giving yourself time to explore, edit, and reflect, you're not just writing, but allowing yourself to develop mastery. You deserve to feel proud of creating your best work, not just throwing it together to get across the finish line.

**Reflect:**
When have you wished for more time to revise, polish, or enjoy a project?

_____

What's one way you could build breathing room into your next writing goal?

_____

**QUICK ACTION**

List two ways you'll remind yourself of these new mindsets during writing sessions (i.e., sticky notes, phone background, calendar alerts):

_____

_____

# your personal mindset reframe

High-pressure habits don't have to run the show. In the space below, create your own personalized mindset reframe that speaks directly to the way your inner Crisis-Maker delays until the pressure is unbearable, and the way your steady writer self learns to act before the alarm bells ring.

## STEP 1: RECOGNIZE THE PATTERN

What is a common thought you have that leads you to delay writing until the last minute? (Example: "I'll get serious once the deadline is closer.")

_____

_____

## STEP 2: WRITE A MORE SUPPORTIVE TRUTH

What new thought will you practice this week to take action before the pressure hits? (Example: "Five minutes today is better than five hours in panic mode.")

_____

_____

## MY STEADY-FOCUS CARD

Use an index card, sticky note, or whatever you like. Write it big, decorate it, or make a small "badge" for your writing space.

**Old thought I'm replacing:** _____

**New thought I'm practicing:** _____

# my hidden rewards

**Urgency gives you a rush, but it comes at a cost.**

Last-minute pressure jolts you into motion. It clears distractions, narrows your focus, and flips a switch that says, "Now or never." In the short term, this can feel thrilling and even productive. But over time, it trains your brain to believe that stress equals creativity, which can make consistent progress feel boring or impossible. By recognizing what your current pattern gives you—and what it takes away—you can begin to shift your momentum from panic-fueled sprints to steady, empowered effort.

## WHAT ARE YOUR HIDDEN REWARDS?

**When I wait until the last minute, I might be getting:** (check all that apply)

☐ A sense of urgency that helps me focus.

☐ Permission to ignore distractions or doubts.

☐ The excuse of "I didn't have time" if it turns out badly.

☐ A feeling of being in the zone creatively.

☐ Relief from having to make long-term plans.

☐ A hit of dopamine from racing the clock.

☐ A sense of identity as someone who works best under pressure.

Other hidden payoffs I've noticed:

_____

_____

_____

_____

**JOURNAL PROMPT**

What have these hidden rewards been costing you creatively, emotionally, and personally? Are you sacrificing quality, peace of mind, or long-term momentum in exchange for that adrenaline-fueled rush?

# future payoffs

You already know how to write under pressure. Now imagine what's possible when you don't have to. What might change if you applied even a fraction of that energy in advance? (Check all that apply.)

**If I stop waiting for a crisis to write, I could gain:**

☐ The calm confidence of steady progress.
☐ The ability to write without burning out.
☐ Higher-quality drafts with less regret and revision.
☐ A writing life that feels more empowering than exhausting.
☐ A better relationship with deadlines and myself.
☐ Time to explore creativity without pressure.
☐ A stronger sense of control and trust in my process.

## OTHER BENEFITS I WANT TO CLAIM

_____     _____

_____     _____

## DESIGN YOUR "MOMENTUM-OVER-MAYHEM" CARD

To be able to make the type of sustained progress a novel requires—or a writing career, for that matter—you'll need to build an identity around consistent motion rather than chaos. Use this space to create a visual or written card that reminds you why steady effort matters. Keep it somewhere visible so when you're tempted to wait for the fire, you'll remember there's a better way.

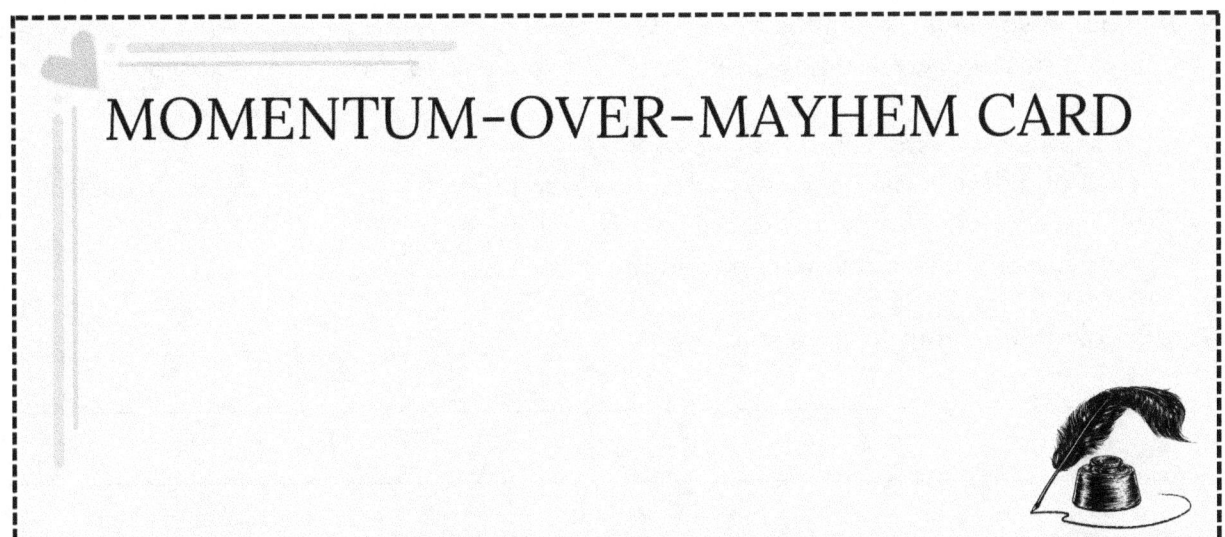

MOMENTUM-OVER-MAYHEM CARD

# your new writer identity

**When urgency drives your writing, it's easy to forget that you have a choice.**

Getting past crisis-mode creativity requires an identity change. The way you see yourself as a writer determines how you behave. When you stop saying "I only write under pressure," and start practicing, "I'm building a writing life that works before the deadline," everything begins to shift. The idea is to see yourself as someone who regularly supports your own health, creativity, and long-term success.

## MY WRITING IDENTITY SHIFT

### Step 1: How do you see yourself now?
Let's be honest: What are the stories you tell yourself when you avoid writing until the last minute? Here are some common Crisis-Maker identity thoughts:

- "I need a deadline to get anything done."
- "I'm only creative when I'm out of time."
- "If it's not urgent, I don't feel motivated."
- "I work best in chaos."

Now, write 3 beliefs, labels, or self-messages you often carry about yourself as a writer.

_____

_____

_____

### Step 2: Who do you want to become?
Now imagine yourself six months from now. You've discovered that showing up early helps you do your best work. What new identity would you love to grow into? Examples:

- "I'm a writer who starts before I 'have to.'"
- "I trust myself to show up, even without a deadline."
- "I've traded panic for peace and my work is stronger for it."
- "I give myself time to revise, rest, and reconnect."

Write 3 beliefs you want to grow into.

_____

_____

_____

**Step 3: What would that version of you do next?**
Next, using the ideas you wrote down, create a simple statement that captures who you are becoming as a writer.

Try this formula:
**Even though I usually _____, I'm learning to _____.**

Here are some examples:

- Even though I usually wait until the last minute, I'm learning to write a little earlier each time.
- Even though I usually rely on adrenaline, I'm learning to pace myself with purpose.
- Even though I usually freeze without pressure, I'm learning to start with one small step even when it's not urgent—or to create that urgency myself!

## MY IDENTITY BRIDGE STATEMENT

_____

_____

_____

## ENCOURAGE YOURSELF!

**Remember:** Every small step you take before the crisis is a radical act of self-leadership. You're not waiting for chaos anymore. Instead, you're choosing to make your writing a regular part of your life, and if you need the pressure, you make it with your own deadlines.

> *I may prefer panic-fueled writing sessions, but I'm learning to power my writing with reliable presence.*

# tools to write without the rush

**If you need a little more pressure, you can create it yourself.**

Crisis-Makers are used to rushing toward deadlines, sprinting through drafts, and "magically" pulling it off last minute. But that constant urgency takes a toll. The key is to work with this hurry-loving part of yourself and find tools that help you stay engaged without the stress. These strategies will help you build energy, structure, and flow before a deadline looms. Start with one or two that spark curiosity. Then feel free to create your own.

## TOOLKIT FOR THE CRISIS-MAKER

### Use a Countdown Calendar

Create a reverse timeline for your next project and highlight mini-deadlines. Visual urgency helps you engage before the panic phase.

### Make Micro-Commitments

Choose one tiny writing action to complete each day, even if it's just 50 words. Momentum builds faster than pressure.

### Use "Deadline Light" Sessions

Set short sessions with a visible timer and a goal. Example: "In the next 20 minutes, I'll write a rough scene." Then stop, no guilt.

### Gamify Progress

Track progress with a system that feels fun with colored checklists, point systems, writing streaks, or rewards for showing up.

### Name the Consequence

Imagine the cost of another last-minute push: missed depth, lost sleep, dropped ideas. Let the truth of the bigger picture inspire change.

### Celebrate Non-Deadline Wins

Notice when you don't need pressure. Celebrate when you write early, prep thoughtfully, or stop before burnout.

### Use Energizing Rituals

Build a pre-writing routine that boosts energy and focus: upbeat music, jumping jacks, or a cold drink to signal "go time."

### Your Turn!

## CHOOSE TWO TOOLS

After reviewing the toolkit, pick two strategies that feel most helpful for you right now. For each one, write a small, clear action step you'll take to practice it this week.

*Examples:*
- If you choose the **Gamify Progress** tool, your action step might be: "Add a gold star to my calendar for every day I write 10 minutes."
- If you choose **Use a Countdown Calendar,** your action step might be: "Break down my short story due next month into 3 mini deadlines and post them above my desk."
- If you choose the **Celebrate Non-Deadline Wins,** your action step might be: "Journal for a week about when I worked without pressure."

## MY TOOLS AND ACTION STEPS

Tool #1 I'm Choosing:

_____

Action Step I'll Take:

_____

Tool #2 I'm Choosing:

_____

Action Step I'll Take:

_____

## THE CRISIS-MAKER'S ANCHOR PHRASE

Instead of thinking you need pressure to be productive, try a powerful anchor, instead. This is a phrase that helps you stay engaged before urgency takes over. Here are some examples:

- "I'm building momentum rather than just chasing deadlines."
- "Urgency doesn't define my value. My focus does."
- "A calm start lets me create something deeper."

**My anchor phrase:**

_____

# mapping your novel journey

**Replace chaos with steady momentum for higher-quality work.**

The key isn't to eliminate your edge, but to retrain it. Small, daily actions—even five focused minutes—build trust, consistency, and breakthroughs before the panic sets in. This week, pick a few micro-steps to try. You'll prove to yourself that you don't need chaos to create something incredible.

## QUICK IDEAS FOR SMALL STEPS

(Choose or modify!)

- Set a 10-minute timer and write one messy paragraph.
- Sketch a fast idea map of your next scene.
- Give yourself one week to revise one chapter. Take the deadline seriously!
- Freewrite what your character wants in this scene in 20 minutes or less.
- Open your draft, highlight your favorite line, then write something new for 5 minutes.
- Write a mini cliffhanger to insert into your next scene.
- List 3 possible endings for your current chapter and employ one in three days.

## MY SMALL STEPS FOR THE WEEK

| Day | One small action... | Did I take it? |
|---|---|---|
| **Monday** | | |
| **Tuesday** | | |
| **Wednesday** | | |
| **Thursday** | | |
| **Friday** | | |
| **Saturday** | | |
| **Sunday** | | |

# NOVEL-WRITING ROADMAP

## Step 1: Start Sooner Than Feels Necessary

- Set a micro-goal today, even if your deadline is far off.
- Make a rough start, like writing 100 words, to break the ice.
- Reward early action to retrain your brain's urgency trigger.

*Example:*
- "I'll give myself 5 minutes to write the first line of the scene, even if I delete it later."
- "I'll sketch a rough version of the chapter arc by Saturday."

**My early start:**

_____

## Step 2: Schedule Creative Pushes Without Panic

- Schedule two 25-minute sprints this week. No delays, no excuses!
- Set up "false deadlines" with a writing buddy or timer.
- End each session with a quick plan for what's next.

*Example:*
- "Write one scene before Wednesday, then celebrate."
- "Create a mini deadline for my Act 1 by Sunday night."

**My focused pushes:**

_____

## Step 3: Build a Sustainable System

- Create a repeatable writing rhythm: 2-3 sessions/week.
- Use low-pressure rituals to trigger writing focus.
- Track your sessions or use an accountability partner to measure consistency.

*Examples:*
- Turn on your favorite playlist and write for 20 minutes 3 days a week.
- Set weekly meetings with your accountability partner to check in on your progress.

**My sustainable system:**

_____

# carry your rhythm forward

**You don't need to crash to create. You just need to keep showing up.**

Your urgency has power, but when you only write under pressure, your creative life becomes a cycle of burnout and recovery. You don't have to completely abandon your intensity. Just find new ways to apply it to your writing routine on a regular basis. Below, you'll find a few examples of how to shift your inner script when the pressure builds. Then, you'll create your own.

## SHIFT YOUR SELF-TALK

| Crisis Thought | Rhythm Reframe |
|---|---|
| "I work best under pressure." | "I work better with momentum." |
| "I can wait—there's still time." | "My deadline for this chapter is tonight!" |
| "I'll just power through later." | "I deserve progress without panic." |
| "Deadlines get me moving." | "I set my own regular deadlines to keep it going." |

### Your Turn

Write down a Crisis-Maker thought and answer with a new rhythm-oriented voice.

| Crisis Thought | Rhythm Reframe |
|---|---|
| | |
| | |
| | |
| | |

**YOUR RHYTHM-RESET PLAN**

**1. What's one phrase I can repeat when I feel the pressure rising again?**
(Example: "Focus isn't a fire drill." or "I don't need panic to produce.")

_____

**2. What's one small ritual I can use to help me begin before urgency takes over?**
(Examples: turn on music, write one sentence, take 5 breaths before typing.)

_____

**3. What's one way I'll acknowledge progress without needing a crisis to earn it?**
(Examples: sticker on a calendar, share one sentence with a friend, take a walk.)

_____

**LOOKING BACK**

Your energy isn't the problem. It's the way you've been abusing it. Every time you show up early, without the panic or pressure, you're proving that you don't have to set fires to find focus. You have the tools now:

- Awareness of your pressure habits.
- Tools to activate focus without chaos.
- A new writer identity that values steadiness.
- Evidence that small steps build real momentum.

# rhythm commitment

> *Rather than be a slave to emergencies, I commit to channeling my creative energy more consistently.*
>
> Signed: _____
>
> Date: _____

# meet the distracted

**You want to write, but your attention has other plans.**

You sit down with the best of intentions, but suddenly you're checking email, scrolling a social media feed, or tackling a "quick" chore. What happened? Your inner distracted writer took over.

In today's noisy world, your brain has adapted to constant interruptions, and focused writing often feels unfamiliar or even uncomfortable. Your attention flits from one tab to the next, chasing novelty instead of staying with the task at hand. Even when you care deeply about your project, staying present long enough to make progress can feel nearly impossible.

But you *can* return to deep-work focus. In this section, you'll learn to work with your distracted mind instead of against it by building structure, minimizing noise, and unlocking the focus your creativity craves.

## COMMON TRAITS OF A DISTRACTED WRITER

- Start writing but quickly drift into checking messages or tabs.
- Feel like everything around you demands your attention.
- Struggle to finish what you start because new ideas constantly pull at you.
- Get overwhelmed by mental clutter or multi-tasking.
- Interrupt yourself to "just do one thing" that turns into many.
- Open your laptop to write . . . and find 45 minutes later you haven't written a word.
- Abandon writing plans for something that feels easier or more urgent.

## SELF-CHECK: DO YOU RECOGNIZE THIS PATTERN?

Check all that apply:
- ☐ I often start a writing session but get pulled away by something else.
- ☐ I find it hard to focus for more than a few minutes at a time.
- ☐ I check my phone, messages, or notifications during writing time.
- ☐ I get excited about new ideas before finishing current ones.
- ☐ I feel like my brain is constantly jumping between tasks.
- ☐ I find it difficult to create quiet or protected time for my writing.
- ☐ I often abandon work when it stops feeling interesting or fun.

# the focus-finding matrix

Whenever your writing momentum shatters, return to this matrix. Skim the rows and columns to find the situation that best fits your current distraction, then immediately take the paired micro-action. No need to "fix" your attention completely. Just gently redirect it.

| When I catch myself... | Then I will... |
|---|---|
| **Drifting into social media** | Turn off notifications and write one sentence. |
| **Chasing a random idea** | Jot it on a sticky note and return to my draft. |
| **Getting up to "do something quickly"** | Set a 5-minute timer and stay put until it dings. |
| **Clicking between too many open tabs** | Close all but one window and focus for 10 minutes. |
| **Bouncing between ideas** | Choose one and commit to it for the next 15 minutes. |
| **Forgetting what I was working on** | Re-read the last paragraph and write the next. |
| **Thinking "I'll come back later"** | Open the document now, even for just a quick glance. |

**JOURNAL PROMPT**

Where does distraction steal your writing time most often? Are there certain triggers—times of day, tasks, or settings—that seem to invite it?

# shift your writing mindset

**Your focus isn't lost. It's just waiting for you.**

You sit down to write, only to check your email. You reread a paragraph, then jump to a new idea. You want to focus, but your attention feels slippery, and every interruption pulls you off course. It's not that you're incapable of focus. It's that you haven't yet built the scaffolding that helps your mind *return* to the task. That starts with shifting how you think about distraction. Instead of beating yourself up or giving up entirely, you'll learn to view attention as a skill you're strengthening.

## MINDSET REFRAME #1

**Old mindset:** "If I can't focus, there's no point in trying."
**New mindset:** "Focus isn't all or nothing. It's something I can return to."
Every time you notice your attention drifting, gently bring it back. Do it again and again. That's how you build mental strength. It doesn't matter how many times you wander. What matters is that you return.

**Reflect:**
When was the last time you abandoned a writing session because you felt too scattered?

_____

What's one way you could gently return to focus next time, even if it's just for 5 minutes?

_____

## MINDSET REFRAME #2

**Old mindset:** "If I were serious, I'd be able to concentrate."
**New mindset:** "Focus is a skill, not a measure of my worth."
Focus is like a muscle you can strengthen with time and repetition. You might need to approach writing differently than others. That doesn't mean you care less. It means you're building a process that works for you.

**Reflect:**
What story have you been telling yourself about your distractions?

_____

How could you reframe that story to include compassion?

_____

**QUICK ACTION**

List two ways you'll actively support your focus this week (i.e., 10-minute timer, clutter-free writing space, single-task sticky note):

_____

_____

# your personal mindset reframe

Changing your mindset means shifting how you respond when focus slips. In the space below, create your own custom reframe. Speak directly to the moments you're most likely to check out, then offer a new, more supportive voice that will call you back in.

## STEP 1: RECOGNIZE THE PATTERN

What thought or habit often knocks you off track?
(Example: "I'll just check one thing first.")

_____

_____

## STEP 2: WRITE A MORE SUPPORTIVE TRUTH

What new thought can guide you gently back to focus?
(Example: "I'll write for 10 minutes first, then decide.")

_____

_____

## MY INNER-FOCUS CARD

Use an index card, sticky note, or whatever you like. Write it big, decorate it, or make a small "badge" for your writing space.

**Old thought I'm replacing:** _____

**New thought I'm practicing:** _____

# my hidden rewards

**Distraction can feel like relief, but it disconnects you from what matters.**

For you, procrastination is often a way to escape the discomfort of creative uncertainty. Switching tasks gives your brain a hit of novelty or productivity, even when it pulls you away from what matters most. Each quick dopamine fix feels good in the moment. But the cost adds up: unfinished work, unmet goals, and a growing sense that you can't trust yourself to follow through. By getting honest about the rewards your distractions are giving you—and the long-term rewards you truly want—you can begin to choose differently.

## WHAT ARE YOUR HIDDEN REWARDS?

**When I distract myself from my writing, I might be getting:** (check all that apply)

☐ A quick burst of dopamine from something more stimulating.

☐ Relief from the discomfort of not knowing what to write.

☐ An escape from the pressure to do things perfectly.

☐ The sense of being "busy" without facing the hard work.

☐ Protection from the fear that my ideas won't be good enough.

☐ A break from sitting still, focusing, or making decisions.

☐ Permission to delay in favor of something that feels easier.

Other hidden payoffs I've noticed:

_____

_____

_____

_____

**JOURNAL PROMPT**

What are these rewards costing you creatively, emotionally, and personally? How would it feel to reclaim your attention for the work that matters most?

# future payoffs

You already know how it feels when distraction takes you away from your writing. Now imagine what's possible when you maintain (or return) your focus. What might change if you got into the habit of bringing your attention back? (Check all that apply.)

**If I practice returning to focus, I could gain:**

☐ Momentum on a project I truly care about.
☐ A deeper connection with my creative voice.
☐ More clarity about what I actually want to create.
☐ A greater sense of accomplishment and self-trust.
☐ The confidence that I can finish what I start.
☐ More meaningful progress with less internal noise.
☐ A calmer, more focused writing practice.

## OTHER BENEFITS I WANT TO CLAIM

_____     _____

_____     _____

## DESIGN YOUR "RETURN-TO-FOCUS" CARD

Your attention is a creative resource that's been stretched thin by a noisy world. But you can reclaim it. To make meaningful progress, you'll need to anchor your writing time in intention, not impulse. Use this space to create a visual or written card that reminds you what focus gives you: clarity, momentum, satisfaction, or even peace. Keep it somewhere visible so when distractions pull at you, you'll remember what you're choosing to return to.

MY RETURN-TO-FOCUS CARD

# your new writer identity

**You're a writer who always returns to what matters.**

When you see yourself as "someone who can't stay focused," you reinforce that belief every time you drift away or get pulled into something else. But identity is a flexible thing. You can build a new one, starting with the smallest returns to your work. Each time you step back toward your writing, you vote for a new version of you: the version who stays. You don't need perfect focus, just a commitment to returning again and again.

## MY WRITING IDENTITY SHIFT

### Step 1: How do you see yourself now?

Let's be honest: What do you believe about yourself as a writer when you're in distraction mode? Here are some common Distracted identity thoughts:

- "I can't stay focused long enough to finish anything."
- "I get bored too fast to stick with one idea."
- "I always abandon projects when they get hard."
- "I'm addicted to scrolling instead of creating."

Now, write 3 beliefs, labels, or self-messages you often carry about yourself as a writer.

_____

_____

_____

### Step 2: Who do you want to become?

Now imagine the version of you who sticks with a project. You're the one who returns even after getting pulled away. What would that writer believe? Examples:

- "I'm a writer who comes back to the page, no matter how many times I drift."
- "I stay with one project long enough to find its soul."
- "I create a space for focus and protect it."
- "I follow through even when the novelty wears off."

Write 3 beliefs you want to grow into.

_____

_____

_____

**Step 3: What would that version of you do next?**
Next, using the ideas you wrote down, create a simple statement that captures who you are becoming as a writer.

Try this formula:
**Even though I usually _____, I'm learning to _____.**

Here are some examples:
- Even though I usually jump to something new, I'm learning to stay just a little longer.
- Even though I usually scroll instead of write, I'm learning to pause and choose the page.
- Even though I usually give up when I get bored, I'm learning to stick with one project long enough to surprise myself.

## MY IDENTITY BRIDGE STATEMENT

_____

_____

_____

## ENCOURAGE YOURSELF!

**Remember:** Every time you resist the scroll, pause the multitask, or return to your draft, you're proving that your attention is something you can reclaim. You're not "bad at focus." You're a writer who's learning to stay.

> # When distraction pulls me away, I'm learning to return— again and again.

# tools to reclaim focus

**Build boundaries that bring your attention back home.**

You can think of distraction as a creativity leak. Your mind wants to make things, but it also seeks novelty, comfort, and stimulation. To solve the problem, all you have to do is adopt some tools that help you write with intention.

The right tools remove temptations and invite you back into the world of your story. By reducing friction, they help you refocus, calm your nervous system, and make your writing space feel like a place you want to be.

## TOOLKIT FOR THE DISTRACTED

### Use a Distraction-Free Timer

Try a Pomodoro-style session: 25 minutes of writing, 5-minute break. No switching tabs. No checking your phone. Just a focused block with a reward at the end.

### Designate a "Focus Zone"

Choose one spot that's only for writing. It could be a specific desk, a cafe table, or even a folder on your laptop. When you enter it, tell your brain, "This is writing time."

### Make a Distraction Parking Lot

Keep a notepad nearby. When a thought or urge arises (check email, look something up, text someone), jot it down. You can come back to it later, after you've written.

### Use Music or Sound Cues

Train your brain to associate a certain sound with writing focus. Create a playlist or use ambient sound apps to cue yourself into the zone.

### Set a Tiny "Return Goal"

Instead of aiming for a long session, challenge yourself to return to your writing five times today, even if it's only for two minutes each.

### Block Digital Temptations

Use website blockers or apps that limit time on social media or news sites while you write. Protect your creative headspace.

### Visualize Your Writing Doorway

Before you start, close your eyes and picture yourself stepping into your story. Feel the door close behind you. You're inside the world now. Let everything else wait.

### Your Turn!

## CHOOSE TWO TOOLS

After reviewing the toolkit, pick two strategies that feel most helpful for you right now. For each one, write a small, clear action step you'll take to practice it this week.

*Examples:*
- If you choose the **Distraction-Free Timer** tool, your action step might be: "Set a timer for 25 minutes and use that time to revise one page."
- If you choose the **Distraction Parking Lot** tool, your action step might be: "Keep a post-it note beside my keyboard and write down every urge that interrupts me."
- If you choose the **Writing Doorway** visualization tool, your action step might be: "Take 30 seconds to visualize my character's world before every session this week."

## MY TOOLS AND ACTION STEPS

Tool #1 I'm Choosing:

_____

Action Step I'll Take:

_____

Tool #2 I'm Choosing:

_____

Action Step I'll Take:

_____

## THE DISTRACTED'S CENTERING PHRASE

Create a small ritual to help you transition from scattered to centered. This doesn't need to be elaborate. All you need is something consistent that tells your brain, "We're here now." Here are some examples:

- "I light my 'focus candle' and breathe deeply before opening my draft."
- "I write one sentence in my notebook before I turn on my computer."
- "I play my writing playlist and close all other tabs."

**My centering phrase:**

_____

# mapping your novel journey

**Learn how to keep your distraction tendencies in line.**

Distraction can be the enemy of writing, but it may also be a part of your creative experience. The key is learning how to manage it so it doesn't mess up your writing routine. This week, practice small moments of return. You don't have to focus perfectly. Just come back to your words again and again.

## QUICK IDEAS FOR SMALL STEPS

(Choose or modify!)

- Open your draft and read one paragraph aloud.
- Make a 3-item "to-write" list and do just one.
- Write a sentence that captures today's feeling.
- Set a 10-minute timer and write anything.
- Use a prompt to freewrite for 5 minutes.
- Re-read a scene and leave one note to your future self.
- Create a "return ritual" and practice it three times this week.

## MY SMALL STEPS FOR THE WEEK

| Day | One small action... | Did I take it? |
|---|---|---|
| Monday | | |
| Tuesday | | |
| Wednesday | | |
| Thursday | | |
| Friday | | |
| Saturday | | |
| Sunday | | |

## NOVEL-WRITING ROADMAP

### Step 1: Lower the friction.

- Leave notes at the end of each session to remind yourself where to start next time.
- Use a sticky note or document title that says: "Start here."
- Create a playlist or sound cue that signals: "It's writing time."

*Example:*
- "Note to self: Next scene opens at the inn. Don't overthink it. Describe the tension."
- "Label a file: Chapter 5—Sketch the fight!"

**My frictionless start:**

_____

### Step 2: Outline in Moments

- Use the "3-beat sketch": Beginning • Twist • Turning Point.
- Keep a running list of "cool scenes" you want to write.
- Summarize a chapter in one sentence while you're on a walk or doing dishes.

*Examples:*
- "Scene ideas: A secret letter arrives. A betrayal is revealed. A chase results."
- "Chapter 7: Character learns their ally has been lying."

**My outline moments:**

_____

### Step 3: Build a Comeback Routine

- Pick 2 short writing windows per week and put them in your calendar.
- Create a pre-writing ritual like a breathing exercise, stretch, or creative spark.
- Write an affirmation that helps you return when distraction pulls you away.

*Examples:*
- "Every Tuesday and Thursday after lunch, I'll write for 20 minutes."
- "I see distraction as a signal to return to my writing."

**My comeback routine:**

_____

# carry your focus forward

**Every day, remind myself: I can regain my focus now.**

Some days, your attention dances in every direction but the page. That means your brain is looking for relief, novelty, or escape. But each time you return to your writing, you train your focus like a muscle. Below are some common Distracted thoughts and how to shift them into a more focused, grounded mindset. After you review these, try creating your own.

## SHIFT YOUR SELF-TALK

| Distracted Thought | Focus Reframe |
| --- | --- |
| "I'll check this one thing first." | "Let's finish one thing before starting another." |
| "I'll write later—this won't take long." | "A few words now is better than none later." |
| "I can't stay focused today." | "I can always return, even for five minutes." |
| "I'll never finish with my attention like this." | "Even scattered steps still count." |

**Your Turn**

Write down a Distracted thought and answer with a new focus-oriented voice.

| Distrated Thought | Focus Reframe |
| --- | --- |
|  |  |
|  |  |
|  |  |
|  |  |

## YOUR RESTORE-YOUR-FOCUS PLAN

**1. What's one phrase I can use to return my attention when I notice I've drifted?**
(Examples: "Back to the page," or "Let's finish this thought first.")

_____

**2. What's one habit I can use to help me focus before or during a writing session?**
(Examples: set a timer, close extra tabs, light a focus candle, use a playlist.)

_____

**3. How will I celebrate my follow-through, especially when focus didn't come easily?**
(Examples: a journal note, a sticker, a YouTube break, sharing your progress)

_____

## LOOKING BACK

You don't need to feel laser-focused to create something meaningful. You just need a rhythm of returning. Every time you ignore the scroll, silence the tab, or close the browser, you're showing your brain what truly matters. You have the tools now:

- Awareness of your attention patterns.
- Tools to anchor your focus.
- A writing identity that includes persistence.
- Evidence that you can return to your work again and again.

# focus commitment

*Despite my mind's desire to wander, I commit to returning to my writing. Each time I come back, I strengthen my ability to finish what I started.*

Signed: _____

Date: _____

# meet the overdoer

**You're doing everything except what matters most.**

You have no shortage of drive. In fact, you often pride yourself on how much you juggle. Your to-do list is never-ending and your days are packed, but the projects that truly matter to you—like your writing—keep getting squeezed out.

You tell yourself you'll get to them once everything else is done. But everything else never ends. As an Overdoer, your procrastination hides behind productivity. You may fear slowing down, saying no, or focusing on one thing because it means facing discomfort, limits, or deeper doubts.

The result? You stay in motion, but your most important writing dreams remain just out of reach. In this chapter, we'll help you slow the spin, refocus your time, and reclaim your energy for what truly matters.

## COMMON TRAITS OF AN OVERDOER WRITER

- Take on too many responsibilities or projects at once.
- Feel uncomfortable resting or saying "no" to others.
- Fill your schedule so full that writing gets pushed out.
- Use productivity to avoid creative uncertainty or discomfort.
- Feel guilty prioritizing your own writing time.
- Say yes to things that drain your writing energy.
- Struggle to identify what truly matters most.

## SELF-CHECK: DO YOU RECOGNIZE THIS PATTERN?

Check all that apply:
- ☐ I often say yes to new obligations before checking if I have time.
- ☐ I avoid my writing by doing other "productive" tasks first.
- ☐ I feel restless or guilty when I try to slow down.
- ☐ I start writing projects but abandon them when I get busy.
- ☐ I rarely protect my writing time from interruptions.
- ☐ I feel most valuable when I'm doing things for others.
- ☐ I crave space for my writing but never seem to get it.

# the boundary-building matrix

Whenever your inner Overdoer starts spinning, pause and come back to this matrix. Scan the rows and pick a stuck moment that sounds familiar. Then immediately take the tiny action beside it. These micro-moves are designed to interrupt the busyness spiral and redirect your attention toward what truly matters: your creative work.

| When I catch myself... | Then I will... |
|---|---|
| Saying "yes" to something that costs me writing time | Say "let me check my calendar" and buy myself space. |
| Putting off writing for chores/errands | Set a timer and write for 5 minutes first. |
| Feeling guilty for prioritizing my writing | Say out loud: "My writing deserves space too." |
| Multitasking while writing session | Shut everything else off and just write. |
| Checking in on others' needs first | Ask myself: "What do I need right now to write?" |
| Filling my schedule without boundaries | Block off my next writing session—no explanations. |
| Saying "it's okay" to not writing | Remember my writing dreams matter! |

**JOURNAL PROMPT**

Where do you most often slip into "overdoing" when it comes to your writing? What do you think is driving that pattern, and what would it feel like to protect your creative space instead?

# shift your writing mindset

**You don't have to earn your right to rest. You already have it.**

You might think, "I'll get to my writing after I handle everything else." But that mindset trains your brain to put your own creative work last. Over time, it drains the joy and meaning from writing altogether. Changing your mindset means challenging the idea that your worth is tied to your productivity. You don't need to be more disciplined or efficient. You need new inner messages that allow you to rest, refuel, and prioritize your deepest creative work.

## MINDSET REFRAME #1

**Old mindset:** "I have to finish everything else before I write."
**New mindset:** "My writing deserves to go first."
When you constantly put writing off to handle other responsibilities, you teach yourself that your dreams come last. Reversing that pattern means recognizing that your writing is a priority. It refuels you and deserves protected time.

**Reflect:**
What's one common task you let take priority over your writing, even when it could wait?

_____

What might change if you protected even 20 minutes for your writing before anything else?

_____

## MINDSET REFRAME #2

**Old mindset:** "If I don't do it all, I'm letting people down."
**New mindset:** "I'm allowed to set limits so I can create."
Writing requires time, attention, and care, just like the people and projects you support. It's not selfish to desire creative space. You're a writer taking your work seriously. Let boundaries become your creative protection.

**Reflect:**
What's one boundary you've been afraid to set around your time?

_____

What could you say "no" to this week to say "yes" to your writing?

_____

**QUICK ACTION**

List two simple ways you'll keep these reframes visible during your writing sessions (i.e., sticky notes, phone background, journal headline):

_____

_____

# your personal mindset reframe

You don't have to "earn" your writing time by doing everything else first. The card below can help you reframe the impulse to overcommit. Let it remind you that honoring your creative work is not a luxury—it's a necessity. When you protect that space, you make room for the writer you're becoming.

## STEP 1: RECOGNIZE THE PATTERN

What thought tends to pull you away from writing and toward "getting more done?"
(Example: "I'll just take care of these five things first.")

_____

_____

## STEP 2: WRITE A MORE SUPPORTIVE TRUTH

What new message can remind you to prioritize your writing?
(Example: "My creative time matters and I'm allowed to protect it.")

_____

_____

**MY CREATIVE-BOUNDARIES CARD**

Use an index card, sticky note, or whatever you like. Write it big, decorate it, or make a small "badge" for your writing space.

**Old thought I'm replacing:** _____

**New thought I'm practicing:** _____

# my hidden rewards

**Your "busyness" is giving you secret payoffs!**

Procrastination isn't always obvious when you're an Overdoer. After all, you're still busy. Overdoing lets you feel accomplished while quietly postponing the hard emotional work of writing. But staying stuck in the cycle of overdoing often means never finishing your writing projects and never seeing what you're truly capable of. By getting honest about the hidden rewards your busyness provides, you can begin to choose differently, bringing more awareness, balance, and intention to each decision you make.

## WHAT ARE YOUR HIDDEN REWARDS?

**When I avoid my writing by staying busy, I might be getting:** (check all that apply)

☐ A sense of usefulness that boosts my self-worth.

☐ An excuse to delay difficult creative decisions.

☐ Temporary escape from the vulnerability writing stirs up.

☐ A way to avoid the fear of finishing and being judged.

☐ Relief from the pressure to make my writing "good enough."

☐ Comfort in doing things I know I'm good at.

☐ A feeling of control, even if I'm not moving forward.

Other hidden payoffs I've noticed:

_____

_____

_____

_____

 **JOURNAL PROMPT**

What have these hidden rewards been costing you emotionally, creatively, or in terms of your writing dreams?

# future payoffs

Imagine what might happen if you gave your energy to the writing that truly matters, rather than scattering it across a thousand tasks. What if instead of chasing productivity, you pursued progress on the project closest to your heart? (Check all that apply.)

**If I choose writing more often, I could:**

☐ Finish a project that's been on your heart for far too long.
☐ Gain clarity about what truly matters in my writing life.
☐ Feel more energy instead of being constantly depleted.
☐ Build trust in my ability to follow through.
☐ Experience real pride in what I complete.
☐ Make visible progress on my long-term writing dreams.
☐ Create time and space for more joy, not just output.

## OTHER BENEFITS I WANT TO CLAIM

_____     _____

_____     _____

## DESIGN YOUR "DO-LESS-CREATE-MORE" CARD

Overdoers tend to fill every moment, chase every opportunity, and stretch themselves too thin. But doing more doesn't always mean creating more. This card is a reminder that your deepest creative impact comes when you slow down, choose wisely, and commit to what truly matters. Use bullet points, statements, quotes, or sketches—whatever inspires clarity and calm. Post it near your writing space as a nudge back to center.

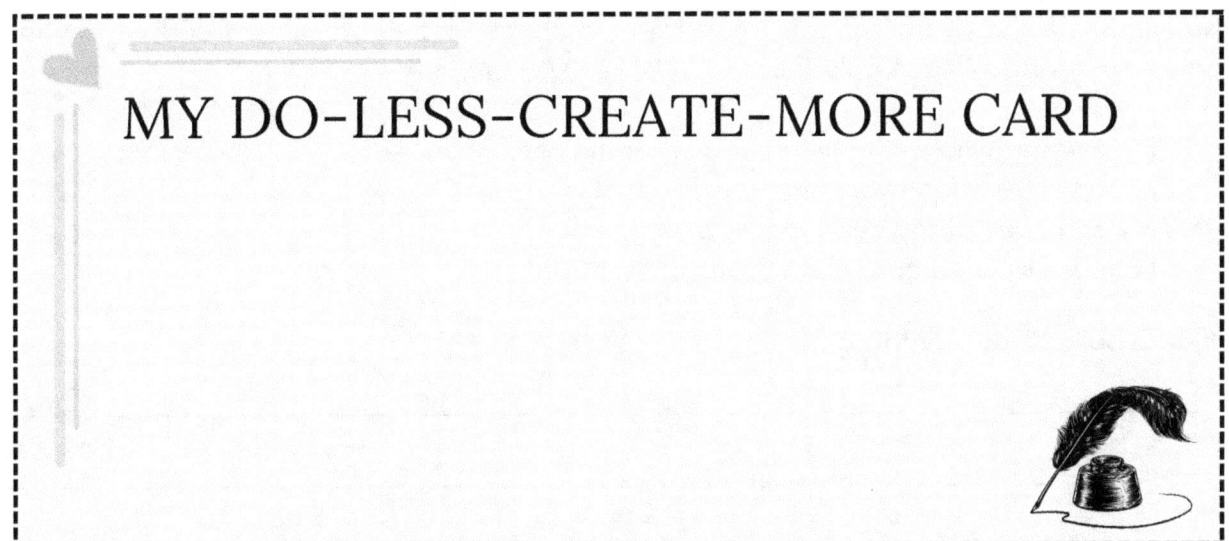

MY DO-LESS-CREATE-MORE CARD

# your new writer identity

**You don't need to prove your worth. You need to protect your creative energy.**

When you think of yourself as someone who must always be productive, helpful, or high-achieving to be "enough," you unknowingly reinforce an identity that leads straight to burnout. When you shift from "I'm a writer who's constantly behind" to "I'm a writer who protects my capacity so I can create what matters," your identity expands to support your dreams. You start making decisions that nourish your creative life instead of draining it.

## MY WRITING IDENTITY SHIFT

### Step 1: How do you see yourself now?

Let's be honest: How do you currently see yourself as a writer when you're overdoing? Here are some common Overdoer identity thoughts:

- "I have to say 'yes' to every opportunity."
- "If I slow down, I'll fall behind."
- "Other people are depending on me. I can't take time to write."
- "There's too much to do to prioritize my creative work."

Now, write 3 beliefs, labels, or self-messages you often carry about yourself as a writer.

_____

_____

_____

### Step 2: Who do you want to become?

Now imagine the version of you who sets boundaries and vigorously defends your writing time and energy. What would that writer believe? Examples:

- "I'm a writer who protects time for what matters most."
- "I don't have to do everything to be valuable."
- "My creative energy deserves my attention."
- "I choose aligned action over constant motion."

Write 3 beliefs you want to grow into.

_____

_____

_____

**Step 3: What would that version of you do next?**
Next, using the ideas you wrote down, create a simple statement that captures who you are becoming as a writer.

Try this formula:
**Even though I usually _____, I'm learning to _____.**

Here are some examples:
- Even though I usually say "yes" to everything, I'm learning to protect my time and focus.
- Even though I usually prioritize others' needs first, I'm learning to honor my creative goals.
- Even though I usually overfill my schedule, I'm learning to choose what truly moves me forward.

## MY IDENTITY BRIDGE STATEMENT

_____

_____

_____

## ENCOURAGE YOURSELF!

**Remember:** Every time you choose to slow down, say no, or do less so you can focus more, that's a vote for the writer you're becoming. You're learning to work in a way that sustains your creative life. Imagine how important that will be when you're looking back on all you've accomplished as a creator!

> *I'm saying "no" more often and choosing to protect the projects that matter most.*

# tools to tame the to-do list

**Help is here to help you choose what matters most!**

When you're an Overdoer, your default setting is everything, all at once. You're juggling multiple writing projects, chasing deadlines, volunteering, networking, researching, tweaking, and still feeling behind. But productivity without intention burns you out and buries your best creative work under busywork.

These tools help you pause, clarify, and prioritize, so your energy flows toward what actually moves your writing forward. The goal is to create filters for yourself and a way to say "no," even to your own pressure.

## TOOLKIT FOR THE OVERDOER

### The 3-Project Rule

Limit your active writing focus to no more than three projects. One major, one minor, and one just for fun.

### Creative "No" List

Write down every writing, marketing, or life task you're tempted to do this week, and then cross off three that aren't essential.

### Completion Corner

Pick one writing task you've been avoiding finishing (a blog post, a scene, a bio). Schedule one session to only work on that.

### Use a Stop-Doing List

You already have a to-do list. Now make a stop-doing list. Write down 3 tasks you'll consciously delay, delegate, or delete this week to reclaim energy for your writing.

### Set a Boundary Session

Block off one non-negotiable writing session this week—no phone, no email, no multitasking, no "quick favors." Protect it like you would an appointment for someone else.

### Reconnect to Your "Why"

When you're constantly serving others, you can forget why your work matters. Spend 5 minutes journaling about why this project is meaningful to you.

### Practice Saying "No"

Choose low-pressure places like stores and restaurants to practice saying "no" without explanation: "No thank you." That's it.

### Your Turn!

## CHOOSE TWO TOOLS

After reviewing the toolkit, pick two strategies that feel most helpful for you right now. For each one, write a small, clear action step you'll take to practice it this week.

*Examples:*
- If you choose **Reconnect to Your Why,** your action step might be: "Journal for 5 minutes tonight on why this project still matters to me."
- If you choose **Use a Stop-Doing List,** your action step might be: "Cross off 3 non-essential tasks from my planner this morning."
- If you choose **Set a Boundary Session,** your action step might be: "Block Friday from 8–8:30 a.m. as protected writing time and mute my phone."

## MY TOOLS AND ACTION STEPS

Tool #1 I'm Choosing:

_____

Action Step I'll Take:

_____

Tool #2 I'm Choosing:

_____

Action Step I'll Take:

_____

## THE OVERDOER'S BOUNDARY MANTRA

Overdoers need boundaries that protect their most meaningful work. Write a short mantra or phrase that anchors you when you're tempted to overcommit, overwork, or overextend. Here are some examples:

- "Busy doesn't equal better."
- "My writing matters enough to deserve space."
- "I don't need to say 'yes' to everything to be enough."

**My boundary mantra:**

_____

# mapping your novel journey

**Give your writing the care you give everyone else.**

You've learned to put everything and everyone else first. Your challenge now is to choose you—to give your real writing projects the same attention you give everything else. These small steps are your reminder that your words are worthy of your energy, time, and presence.

## QUICK IDEAS FOR SMALL STEPS

(Choose or modify!)

- Say "no" to a request that steals energy from your writing.
- Choose one task on your writing to-do list to delete.
- Spend 15 minutes on your most important project—not the "urgent" one.
- Journal about one way you've neglected your writing and how you'll change that.
- Revisit your creative "why" and write one sentence that reminds you.
- Delay a chore or errand to make space for your next scene.
- Block 30 minutes this week that belong only to you and your writing.

## MY SMALL STEPS FOR THE WEEK

| Day | One small action... | Did I take it? |
|---|---|---|
| Monday | | |
| Tuesday | | |
| Wednesday | | |
| Thursday | | |
| Friday | | |
| Saturday | | |
| Sunday | | |

## NOVEL-WRITING ROADMAP

### Step 1: Focus your fire.

- Pick one idea to prioritize (even if others are "waiting in the wings").
- Write a list of reasons why this idea or story is important to you.
- Say "no" to 2-3 writing tasks that don't support this story.

*Example:*
- "I'm choosing to finish my historical novel because it still excites me."
- "I owe this story a real chance before I jump to make someone else happy."

### My focused-fire start:

_____

### Step 2: Build a Realistic Outline

- Start with one project only. Outline just the idea you're committed to finishing.
- Outline no more than 5 core story beats to avoid overwhelm.
- Limit your outlining time to 15-20 minutes so you don't burn out before you begin.

*Examples:*
- "Focus only on the novel about the musician, not the series idea or side project."
- "Opening ➜ Major setback ➜ Turning point ➜ Climax ➜ Resolution."

### My realistic outline:

_____

### Step 3: Create Protected Novel Time

- Block one weekly "novel session" that can't be bumped for busywork or obligations.
- Set a pre-session ritual to help you transition from helper mode to creator mode.
- Track your progress with stars, checkmarks, or something visual.

*Examples:*
- "Wednesday night is novel night. No errands, no email, no multitasking."
- "Light a candle and write 250 words. That's my contract with myself."

### My protected novel routine:

_____

# carry your boundaries forward

**There's magic in limiting your focus and energy to only a few projects.**

You're the one others count on—the helper, the doer, the one who always follows through. Now it's your turn. The writing that matters to you deserves your time and attention. You're allowed to invest your energy in work that restores you, not just work that serves everyone else. Below are common Overdoer thoughts and how to shift them into a more self-honoring mindset. Review these, then create your own.

## SHIFT YOUR SELF-TALK

| Overdoer Thought | Boundary Reframe |
|---|---|
| "I can't write until I finish everything else." | "My writing matters too, and it doesn't have to wait." |
| "I'll just do this quick task first." | "Quick tasks add up. I choose my priorities." |
| "I feel guilty writing when others need me." | "I need to make myself as important as others." |
| "I said 'yes,' so I have to go." | "I can change my mind to protect my energy." |

### Your Turn
Write down an Overdoer thought and answer with a new boundary-focused voice.

| Overdoer Thought | Boundary Reframe |
|---|---|
|  |  |
|  |  |
|  |  |
|  |  |

**YOUR SET-BOUNDARIES PLAN**

**1. What should I say to myself when I feel pulled to "just do one more thing?"**
(Example: "My writing doesn't come last.")

_____

**2. What's one boundary I'll set this week to protect my writing session?**
(Examples: No email before writing. Phone off. Door closed.)

_____

**3. What's one way I'll reward myself for showing up, even if it's just for 15 minutes?**
(Examples: Marking a tracker, sharing progress with a friend, five minutes of quiet time.)

_____

**LOOKING BACK**

You are allowed to write without first saving the world. You are allowed to rest, say "no" and focus your fire. Those old patterns—overpromising, overcommitting, overhelping—may still tug at you now and then. But now you have something new:

- Clarity about what really matters.
- Tools to simplify and refocus.
- A writing identity that includes boundaries.
- A renewed commitment to your dreams.

# boundaries commitment

> ## I commit to honoring my time, energy, and creative work by choosing what matters most and following through.

Signed: _____

Date: _____

# meet the guilty

**You don't owe penance. You deserve a fresh start.**

When you're a Guilty writer, the weight of regret hangs over your creative life. It's not just that you've procrastinated—it's that you know you've procrastinated, and you carry the shame of it everywhere you go. Instead of shrugging off your delays, you berate yourself for them. You replay your failures in your mind and tell yourself you should be doing more, achieving more, making up for lost time.

Ironically, this self-reproach only worsens the problem. Instead of motivating you, your guilt turns into quicksand, trapping you in a painful cycle of shame and avoidance. Even when you manage to sit down to write, you may find yourself distracted by thoughts of what you didn't do yesterday, last month, or even last year.

It's time to change the script. Guilt isn't proof that you're failing. It's proof that your writing matters to you. In this section, you'll learn how to stop dragging your past behind you and reclaim your writing future, one small, healing step at a time.

## COMMON TRAITS OF A GUILTY WRITER

- Feel consumed by regret over missed writing sessions or deadlines.
- Judge yourself harshly for your past procrastination.
- Compare yourself to others and feel like you'll never catch up.
- Tell yourself you don't deserve success because you haven't earned it yet.
- Push yourself too hard to "make up for lost time," then burn out.
- See writing more as a duty than a joy.
- Feel too ashamed to go back to abandoned projects.

## SELF-CHECK: DO YOU RECOGNIZE THIS PATTERN?

Check all that apply:
- ☐ I often replay past writing failures in my head.
- ☐ I tell myself I'm always behind and need to catch up.
- ☐ I feel ashamed when I think about how much I haven't written.
- ☐ I believe I've wasted too much time to be successful now.
- ☐ I avoid writing because I fear confirming I've "lost it."
- ☐ I try to do too much at once to make up for lost time.
- ☐ I rarely celebrate progress because it never feels like enough.

# the guilt-recovery matrix

Whenever your guilt flares up, pause and come back to this matrix. Find the description that fits your stuck moment, then take the small paired action. Use these to interrupt the spiral and remind yourself: you're allowed to begin again any time you need to. There is no shame in that.

| When I catch myself... | Then I will... |
| --- | --- |
| **Beating myself up for past procrastination** | Take 5 minutes to write anything today just to remind myself I still can. |
| **Thinking I've wasted too much time** | Write one kind sentence to myself in my journal. |
| **Comparing myself to more "disciplined" writers** | Close social media and write 3 sentences of my own story. |
| **Avoiding a project I abandoned** | Open the file and read one paragraph without pressure to change anything. |
| **Feeling I don't deserve success** | List 3 ways I've shown up for my writing. |
| **Feeling like it's "too late"** | Set a timer for 10 minutes and just reconnect with a scene or idea I love. |
| **Saying "it's okay" to not writing** | Remember my writing dreams matter! |

**JOURNAL PROMPT**

Where do you most often get stuck in guilt? Is it about missed deadlines, unfinished drafts, or comparing yourself to others? What would it feel like to forgive yourself for just one of those things?

# shift your writing mindset

**Guilt doesn't fuel your writing. Instead, it quietly empties your tank.**

Your mindset is often shaped by the past. You tell yourself you should have written more by now, shouldn't have abandoned that project, or should been more disciplined. You may feel like you're motivating yourself, but you're not. You're shaming yourself, and shame rarely leads to sustained creative progress. The shift starts when you start giving yourself permission to return as you are. Your stories don't need a perfect writer. They just need you to come back.

## MINDSET REFRAME #1

**Old mindset:** "I've wasted too much time."
**New mindset:** "Writers come back. That's what makes them writers."
Guilt ties your identity to what you didn't do, but you don't have to "make up" for lost time. Every time you sit down, even for five minutes, you're creating something far more powerful than shame: self-trust.

**Reflect:**
When have you let guilt keep you from returning to something that mattered to you?

_____

What's one way you could reclaim a piece of your writing life this week?

_____

## MINDSET REFRAME #2

**Old mindset:** "I need to make up for all the time I lost."
**New mindset:** "I can begin again today."
Gentle consistency creates a new experience of yourself as a writer, one that's rooted in care instead of criticism. Let your progress be quiet, soft, and steady. One step today. One step tomorrow. Make each step easy!

**Reflect:**
What pressure do you put on yourself to "catch up?" How has that affected your writing?

_____

What's one small action that feels like healing, not punishment?

_____

## QUICK ACTION

List two small ways you'll remind yourself of these new mindsets this week
(i.e., sticky notes, calendar reminders, mantras in your notebook):

_____

_____

# your personal mindset reframe

Guilt thrives in silence, but a single compassionate statement can break its hold. In this activity, you'll name the guilt-thought that holds you back, then rewrite it as a truth you're learning to live by.

## STEP 1: RECOGNIZE THE PATTERN

What's a thought you often have that brings up guilt about your writing?
(Example: "I'm behind and I'll never catch up.")

_____

_____

## STEP 2: WRITE A GENTLER TRUTH

What message could help you return with self-respect instead of shame?
(Example: "My writing life starts fresh every time I return.")

_____

_____

### MY FRESH-START CARD

Use an index card, sticky note, or whatever you like. Write it big, decorate it, or make a small "badge" for your writing space.

**Old thought I'm replacing:** _____

**New thought I'm practicing:** _____

# my hidden rewards

**Guilt may seem punishing, but it can also serve as protection.**

For Guilty writers, procrastination is often tied to deep emotional patterns of self-blame, regret, or the belief that writing is a luxury you haven't earned. On the surface, it may look like you're disciplining yourself. But underneath, you might be avoiding the pain of feeling like you don't deserve the joy of creating. Guilt holds you back by convincing you that something else (or someone else) should come first. When you start recognizing the hidden emotional rewards you're getting from this pattern, you can begin to rewrite the script.

## WHAT ARE YOUR HIDDEN REWARDS?

**When I avoid my writing because of guilt, I might be getting:** (check all that apply)

☐ A sense of control by "punishing" myself for past inconsistency.

☐ Relief from the pressure to prove I'm still "a real writer."

☐ Temporary ease by prioritizing others instead of myself.

☐ Permission to avoid the role of creator.

☐ Escape from facing emotions I've attached to my writing.

☐ Protection from the vulnerability of sharing my voice again.

☐ A delay in confronting the grief of projects I've abandoned.

Other hidden payoffs I've noticed:

_____

_____

_____

_____

 **JOURNAL PROMPT**

What has guilt helped you avoid in your writing life, and what has it cost you creatively, emotionally, and personally?

# future payoffs

Now imagine what might happen if you stopped trying to make up for lost time and simply allowed yourself to begin again. What if showing up, no matter how imperfectly, was enough? (Check all that apply.)

**If I release guilt and return to writing more often, I might gain:**

☐ A renewed sense of connection to my creative self.
☐ Proof that I can follow through again.
☐ Joy in expressing myself without pressure or shame.
☐ A peaceful rhythm of writing that supports me.
☐ Confidence that I still have something to say.
☐ Closure around old projects that still matter to me.
☐ The freedom to create without apology.

## OTHER BENEFITS I WANT TO CLAIM

_____    _____

_____    _____


## DESIGN YOUR "PERMISSION-TO-BEGIN" CARD

Guilt convinces you that you don't deserve a fresh start. But you do. Creating a visual reminder of your right to write can help interrupt those old messages and remind you: returning to writing is always allowed. It's not about what you've done or haven't done. It's about what you're choosing now.

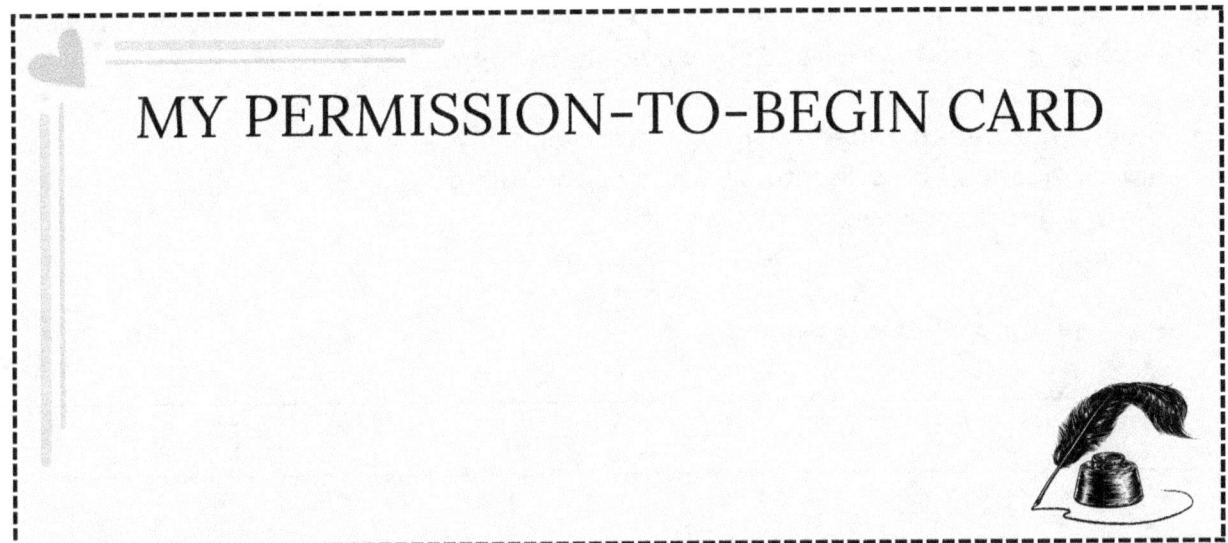

MY PERMISSION-TO-BEGIN CARD

# your new writer identity

**You don't need to "make up" for the past.**

When guilt defines your writing identity, every missed deadline, shelved project, or abandoned draft becomes a source of shame. You may start thinking of yourself as unreliable, inconsistent, or unworthy of calling yourself a writer. But those thoughts only deepen your disconnection. Instead, believe that you're allowed to begin again. Rewrite the story you tell yourself. You're a resilient writer who returns to get the work done, no matter what's happened before.

## MY WRITING IDENTITY SHIFT

### Step 1: How do you see yourself now?

Let's be honest: How do you currently see yourself as a writer today?  Here are some common Guilty identity thoughts:

- "I'm the kind of writer who always lets myself down."
- "I've abandoned too many projects to be a real writer."
- "I missed my chance to make something meaningful."
- "I don't deserve to write until I fix everything I've left undone."

Now, write 3 beliefs, labels, or self-messages you often carry about yourself as a writer.

_____

_____

_____

### Step 2: Who do you want to become?

Now imagine you've become a writer who shows up for your writing with forgiveness, consistency, and gentle resolve. What would that writer believe? Examples:

- "Each time I return, I strengthen trust in myself."
- "I don't need to be perfect to be worthy of creating."
- "My words matter, even if they arrive late."
- "I'm learning to write with love, not punishment."

Write 3 beliefs you want to grow into.

_____

_____

_____

## Step 3: What would that version of you do next?

Next, using the ideas you wrote down, create a simple statement that captures who you are becoming as a writer.

Try this formula:
**Even though I usually _____, I'm learning to _____.**

Here are some examples:
- Even though I usually beat myself up for not writing, I'm learning to meet myself with compassion and start anyway.
- Even though I usually avoid projects I've neglected, I'm learning that returning is a strength, not a failure.
- Even though I usually feel behind, I'm learning that every word I write still counts.

## MY IDENTITY BRIDGE STATEMENT

_____

_____

_____

## ENCOURAGE YOURSELF!

**Remember:** Every act of return is an act of renewal. The more often you meet yourself with care instead of punishment, the more writing becomes a place of possibility again. You don't have to make up for lost time. Just start from where you are.

> # My guilt doesn't define me. My willingness to return does.

# tools to reclaim your writing

**Let guilt be a signal, not a sentence.**

Guilt thrives in silence. When you avoid your writing for a while, then try to return, that familiar shame gremlin shows up: *You should have done more. You're so behind. Why even try?* The longer you stay away, the meaner it gets.

To quiet this gremlin, you need compassionate tools that meet you where you are. The ones on these pages are designed to help you reconnect without pressure, and rebuild your writing rhythm step by step. Look them over, then create your own.

## TOOLKIT FOR THE GUILTY

### The 5-Minute Welcome Back Session

Instead of trying to "catch up," just open your project and set a timer for 5 minutes. Write anything. Remind yourself: This is enough to start.

### The Forgiveness Sticky Note

Write a compassionate message to yourself and stick it near your writing space. Examples: "I'm allowed to return without shame." Or "Guilt is not required to begin."

### Write a "Reunion" Entry

Journal for 10 minutes as if you're reuniting with your story. Ask: What have you missed? What's been waiting for you?

### Create a "Return Playlist"

Choose 3-5 songs that help you feel connected, hopeful, or grounded. Play them each time you begin a session.

### Track Heart, Not Hustle

Instead of measuring words or hours, track the emotional win. Did you show up with honesty? Did you stay for 10 minutes? That counts.

### Use a Shame-Softening Phrase

Choose a phrase to whisper when guilt tries to take over. Example: "I don't have to be perfect. I can just be present."

### The Guilt Drop-Off Station

Grab a sticky note and scribble down the guilty thought that's been nagging you. Toss it in a jar or even a laundry basket. Turn letting go into a moment of relief.

### Your Turn!

## CHOOSE TWO TOOLS

After reviewing the toolkit, pick two strategies that feel most helpful for you right now. For each one, write a small, clear action step you'll take to practice it this week.

*Examples:*
- If you choose the **5-Minute Welcome Back** tool, your action step might be: "Set a timer and write anything in my draft for 5 minutes—no expectations."
- If you choose the **Forgiveness Sticky Note** tool, your action step might be: "Write a kind message to myself and post it near my writing space today."
- If you choose the **Return Playlist** tool, your action step might be: "Make a 3-song playlist that helps me feel hopeful and play it before each session."

## MY TOOLS AND ACTION STEPS

Tool #1 I'm Choosing:

_____

Action Step I'll Take:

_____

Tool #2 I'm Choosing:

_____

Action Step I'll Take:

_____

## THE GUILTY'S WELCOME PHRASE

You need a welcome sign to bring you back to your writing. Create a phrase you'll say to yourself each time you return to your work, especially after time away. Here are some examples:

- "It's okay to begin again."
- "This page doesn't care how long I've been gone."
- "I return with love, not punishment."

**My welcome phrase:**

_____

# mapping your novel journey

**Return gently. Restore your rhythm. Reclaim your voice.**

When guilt has kept you away from your writing, even small steps can feel like a stretch. Don't try to make up for lost time. Just do your best to begin again, kindly, consistently, and without punishment. Every time you choose to return, you're proving to yourself that your voice still matters.

## QUICK IDEAS FOR SMALL STEPS

(Choose or modify!)

- Open your draft and write one new sentence just to reconnect.
- Revisit a scene you used to love and read it aloud.
- Freewrite for 5 minutes about why this story still matters to you.
- Add a single line of dialogue to your current project.
- Create a writing ritual that welcomes you back without pressure.
- Journal about what guilt has taught you and what you're ready to let go of.
- Make a short "return-to-writing" playlist and play it before each session.

## MY SMALL STEPS FOR THE WEEK

| Day | One small action... | Did I take it? |
|---|---|---|
| Monday | | |
| Tuesday | | |
| Wednesday | | |
| Thursday | | |
| Friday | | |
| Saturday | | |
| Sunday | | |

## NOVEL-WRITING ROADMAP

### Step 1: Re-enter without punishment.

- Revisit a scene or idea that excites you. Don't worry if it's not where you "should" be.
- Set a tiny goal for your session. (Example: "Write 50 words.")
- Choose a location or ritual that helps shift your mindset from guilt to permission.

*Example:*
- "I'll reread the first paragraph of my draft, and write one new line just to get going."
- "I'll set a timer for 10 minutes and let myself ramble in my story journal."

### My non-punishing re-entry:

_____

### Step 2: Reset with a Gentle Outline

- Sketch out an outline that seems "fun" for you—no pressure.
- Jot down 3–5 story beats you're excited to explore.
- List a few character or emotional arcs that still interest you.

*Examples:*
- "This is a story about forgiveness, and I want to capture that emotion."
- "Next scenes: character faces her past • opens up to friend • takes a risk."

### My gentle outline:

_____

### Step 3: Rebuild a Guilt-Free Routine

- Choose one low-pressure writing session per week where showing up is the only goal.
- Design a ritual that offers emotional reassurance.
- Create a gentle way to track progress, one that affirms consistency, not perfection.

*Examples:*
- "Before writing, I'll place my dad's bookmark next to me. It reminds me this matters."
- "I'll purchase a calendar I like specifically for tracking my writing time."

### My guilt-free routine:

_____

# carry your compassion forward

**Guilt thrives on the past. But your power lies in the present.**

You don't owe your creativity a flawless track record. What matters is how you speak to yourself today. Every time you return to your writing with self-compassion, you teach your brain that you are allowed to move forward without shame. Below are some common Guilty Writer thoughts, and how to reframe them with more kindness and clarity.

## SHIFT YOUR SELF-TALK

| Guilty Thought | Compassion Reframe |
|---|---|
| "I've wasted too much time." | "Every day I return is a fresh start." |
| "I should be further along by now." | "My path unfolds at my pace." |
| "I can't focus. I've let myself down." | "I can choose to focus now, with care." |
| "I don't deserve to write if I keep quitting." | "I'm a writer because I keep coming back to writing. That proves it matters to me." |

### Your Turn

Write down a Guilty thought and answer with a new compassion-oriented voice.

| Guilty Thought | Compassion Reframe |
|---|---|
|  |  |
|  |  |
|  |  |
|  |  |

**YOUR COMPASSION-INSPIRED PLAN**

**1. What's one thing I want to tell myself next time guilt rises?**
(Example: "I don't owe the past a punishment. I'm here now.")

_____

**2. What's one symbol or ritual I'll use to re-enter writing with compassion?**
(Examples: wearing a special "writing ring," reading one page from your favorite book.)

_____

**3. What's one way I'll honor my effort—without guilt—after I write?**
(Examples: a gentle walk, a warm drink, reading a kind note you wrote to yourself.)

_____

**LOOKING BACK**

Letting go of guilt is not weakness—it's wisdom. The writer you are becoming is defined by your willingness to return with honesty, care, and a commitment to keep trying. And now you have something new:

- Awareness of the guilt patterns that hold you back.
- Tools to release shame and re-enter your work gently.
- A new writing identity rooted in grace, not punishment.
- Proof that you can begin again without apology.

# compassion commitment

> *I choose to treat myself with kindness as I return to my writing. Each time I show up, I am affirming my worth.*

Signed: _____

Date: _____

# meet the disorganized

**When your space and time support you, progress becomes possible.**

As a Disorganized writer, your creativity isn't the problem. You've got plenty of ideas. The trouble starts when you try to keep track of them. You might misplace files, lose your outline, or forget what you were working on last. Tasks pile up, your workspace gets chaotic, and just figuring out where to begin feels overwhelming. Without a way to manage your time, tools, or ideas, you end up procrastinating not because you're unmotivated, but because you feel buried under the mess.

You may also avoid returning to a project simply because it's disorganized, and that avoidance only makes the chaos worse. Over time, this creates a cycle: the more disorganized things feel, the more you put them off. And the more you put them off, the more scattered they become.

This chapter will help you interrupt that cycle, create just enough structure to support your process, and follow through on the writing that matters most.

## COMMON TRAITS OF A DISORGANIZED WRITER

- Have a dozen half-started projects scattered across notebooks, docs, or apps.
- Struggle to find or remember where you saved your latest draft.
- Jump between ideas without a clear sense of priority or order.
- Forget deadlines, or create unrealistic ones and then miss them.
- Start a new idea before completing the one you're working on.
- Feel overwhelmed by messy files, jumbled notes, or cluttered workspaces.
- Have trouble knowing what to do next when you sit down to write.

## SELF-CHECK: DO YOU RECOGNIZE THIS PATTERN?

Check all that apply:
- ☐ I often have trouble finishing projects I've started.
- ☐ I lose track of my progress or can't find what I worked on last.
- ☐ I have ideas, but I rarely follow them through to completion.
- ☐ My writing space (physical or digital) is chaotic or overwhelming.
- ☐ I bounce between multiple projects and struggle to stay focused.
- ☐ I feel like I'm always writing, but never getting anything done.
- ☐ I rarely take time to pause, organize, or make a plan.

# the find-your-footing matrix

When everything feels scattered, this matrix can help you re-center. Look down the left-hand column to name what's tripping you up. Then follow the small action on the right to steady yourself and take one doable next step. You don't need to fix the whole system. Just interrupt the spiral with one clear move.

| When I catch myself... | Then I will... |
|---|---|
| **Opening five projects at once** | Pick one and set a 15-minute timer just for that. |
| **Looking for the "perfect" file** | Create a new one. Progress matters more than finding. |
| **Avoiding my messy outline** | Jot down 3 bullet points of what I do know. |
| **Starting something new (again)** | Set a reminder to revisit my current draft today. |
| **Forgetting where I left off** | Leave myself a "start here" note at the end of each session. |
| **Feeling overwhelmed by clutter** | Clear just one part of my space—desk, doc, or folder. |
| **Jumping between too many projects** | Choose one to focus on today and set the rest aside (physically or digitally). |

**JOURNAL PROMPT**

Where does disorganization show up most in your writing life? Brainstorming? Drafting? Managing files? What's one area you'd love to bring a little more clarity or flow to?

# shift your writing mindset

**All you have to do is make space for what matters.**

Your mindset may be focused on capturing every idea, staying in motion, or doing what feels urgent in the moment. Without some structure, your ideas and your confidence can begin to unravel. Changing your mindset means acknowledging that a bit of clarity and follow-through can help you harness your natural creativity, but you don't need a flawless system or to follow someone else's organizational plan. You just need something that works well enough to help you finish.

## MINDSET REFRAME #1

**Old mindset:** "I can't focus until everything is sorted."
**New mindset:** "One small action brings more clarity than waiting for complete order."
Waiting for everything to feel "in place" keeps you stuck. Progress doesn't require tidiness, necessarily. You just need a little bit of direction. When you take one small step, even in a mess, you begin building a path forward.

**Reflect:**
What's one writing task you've put off because you felt too scattered to begin?

_____

Even if you've got a mess around you, what's one tiny move you could make just to start?

_____

## MINDSET REFRAME #2

**Old mindset:** "I never stick to a system, so I must not be a real writer."
**New mindset:** "I don't need a perfect system. I need one step I can repeat."
Writing doesn't require flawless systems. What you need is one small step that works for you, and the self-trust to return to it again and again. Consistency is built through rhythm, not rigidity.

**Reflect:**
What's one low-stress writing step you have repeated in the past, even if inconsistently?

_____

How might you build on that instead of scrapping it for something new?

_____

## QUICK ACTION

List two small ways you'll remind yourself of these new mindsets this week (i.e., sticky note reminder, end-of-session "start here" marker, folder cleanup):

_____

_____

# your personal mindset reframe

You don't have to turn yourself into a planner-perfect, color-coding machine. Your way of working can still work. In the space below, create your own mindset reframe that speaks directly to the way your inner Disorganized writer gets overwhelmed, and how your creative self can gently respond with structure that supports you.

## STEP 1: RECOGNIZE THE PATTERN

What's a common thought you have that leads you to feel disorganized or scattered? (Example: "I can't stay organized, so I'll never finish.")

_____

_____

## STEP 2: WRITE A MORE SUPPORTIVE TRUTH

What new thought will you practice this week to honor how you work best? (Example: "I can create systems that support me, even if they look different than everyone else's.")

_____

_____

### MY SYSTEM-FRIENDLY MINDSET CARD

Use an index card, sticky note, or whatever you like. Write it big, decorate it, or make a small "badge" for your writing space.

**Old thought I'm replacing:** _____

**New thought I'm practicing:** _____

# my hidden rewards

**Disorganization feels familiar, but it keeps you tangled.**

For you, procrastination can serve as a coping tool. When you avoid your draft, you also avoid facing the mess. You don't have to confront the scattered notes, the half-finished outlines, the to-do lists you've lost track of. And for a little while, that feels like relief. But avoiding the stress only allows it to build up. And the longer you wait, the heavier it gets. Naming the hidden payoffs of this pattern can help you start to build writing habits that are light, doable, and tailored to your unique mind.

### WHAT ARE YOUR HIDDEN REWARDS?

**When I avoid my writing, I might be getting:** (check all that apply)

☐ Relief from having to face the clutter or disorganization.

☐ An excuse not to finish something I've lost track of.

☐ Escape from decisions I don't feel prepared to make.

☐ Protection from the pressure to suddenly "be organized."

☐ The comfort of familiar chaos—it's what I know.

☐ Temporary freedom from stress, even if it's short-lived.

☐ A way to postpone feelings of guilt or inadequacy.

Other hidden payoffs I've noticed:

_____

_____

_____

_____

**JOURNAL PROMPT**

What has procrastination helped you avoid facing, and how has that impacted your confidence as a writer? What small part of your writing life might feel lighter if you faced it gently?

# future payoffs

Now imagine you start showing up for your writing, even in the middle of chaos. Over time, this builds something powerful: momentum, trust, and clarity. What might you gain from that sort of approach? (Check all that apply.)

**If I show up for my writing—mess and all—I could gain:**

☐ Relief from the guilt of always falling behind.
☐ More clarity about what I'm working on and why.
☐ A simple structure that helps me stay grounded.
☐ Confidence in my ability to finish something.
☐ A creative rhythm that works with my real life.
☐ A sense of pride in how far I've come.
☐ A toolbox that helps me manage my scattered energy.

## OTHER BENEFITS I WANT TO CLAIM

_____    _____

_____    _____

## DESIGN YOUR "WORK-MY-WAY" CARD

As a Disorganized writer, it's easy to compare yourself to people with perfect planners and color-coded outlines. But that doesn't help you. In the space below, create a small reminder card that reflects how you work best. Use bullet points, short affirmations, or doodles—whatever helps you remember that your path is valid and your steps count. Keep it visible in your writing space or inside your notebook.

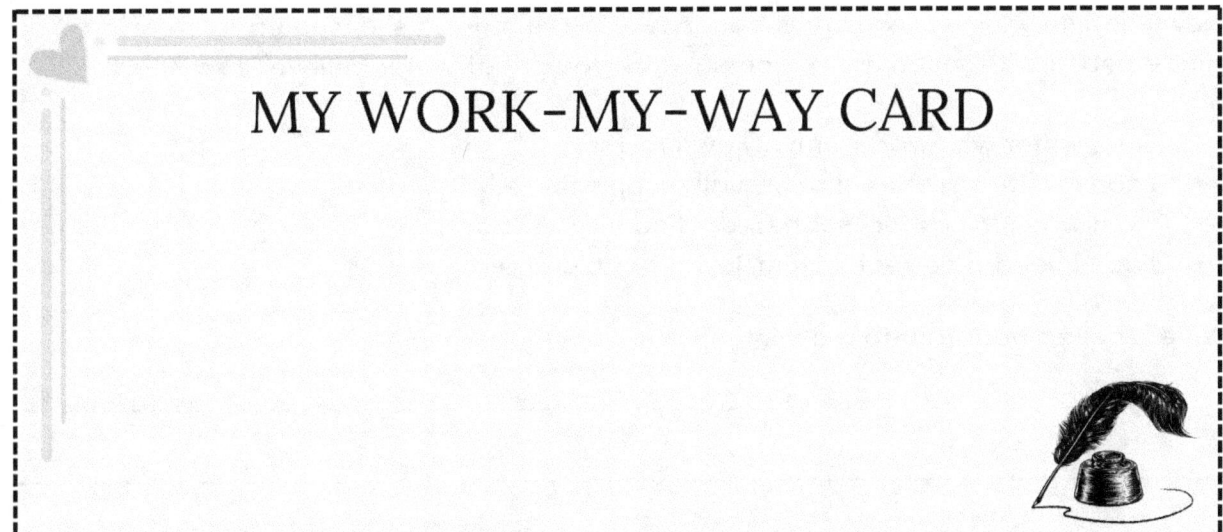

MY WORK-MY-WAY CARD

# your new writer identity

**If you can see yourself as someone who gets the work done, you'll change.**

When you see yourself as someone who "just can't get it together," you start to believe that real writing success is out of reach. You might joke about your chaos, or quietly criticize yourself for being unreliable, messy, or inconsistent. Shifting your identity starts with refusing to define yourself by your disorder. When you start seeing yourself as a writer who can adapt, experiment, and keep showing up in your own way, everything changes.

## MY WRITING IDENTITY SHIFT

### Step 1: How do you see yourself now?
Let's get honest. What do you tend to believe about yourself when you struggle to stay on top of your writing? Here are some common Disorganized identity thoughts:

- "I'm a mess. No wonder I can't finish anything."
- "I always lose track of where I was."
- "If I can't do it consistently, it doesn't count."
- "I never stick with one thing long enough."

Now, write 3 beliefs, labels, or self-messages you often carry about yourself as a writer.

_____

_____

_____

### Step 2: Who do you want to become?
Now imagine yourself six months from now. You've started showing up more often. You've made peace with your messy process. What would that writer believe? Examples:

- "I'm a writer who works with my own rhythms."
- "I can create structure that actually supports me."
- "Even when things feel scattered, I find my way back."
- "I don't need a perfect system, just a doable one."

Write 3 beliefs you want to grow into.

_____

_____

_____

### Step 3: What would that version of you do next?

Next, using the ideas you wrote down, create a simple statement that captures who you are becoming as a writer.

Try this formula:

**Even though I usually _____, I'm learning to _____.**

Here are some examples:
- Even though I usually jump from project to project, I'm learning to finish one thing at a time.
- Even though I usually lose track of where I am, I'm learning to use check-ins that help me return.
- Even though I usually feel scattered, I'm learning to keep moving no matter the "mess" around me.

## MY IDENTITY BRIDGE STATEMENT

_____

_____

_____

## ENCOURAGE YOURSELF!

**Remember:** Every step you take to organize your writing life in your own way is a step toward trusting yourself again. They key is to find what works for you and do more of that. Experiment on your own. Try something. If it works, great! If not, move to something else. Gradually, you will create your own organizational system.

> # *I may not organize like other people, but I'm discovering the systems that fit me.*

# tools to finish what you start

**Allow yourself to make small changes one at a time.**

Disorganized writers often have no shortage of ideas for writing projects. What's missing is the follow-through. With too many tabs open (mentally or literally), it's easy to lose track of where you are, what matters most, or how to return to something after life pulls you away.

You can't expect yourself to simply change overnight, though. These tools help you create your own light-touch systems so your writing can stop getting buried under chaos, clutter, and good intentions.

## TOOLKIT FOR THE OVERDOER

### The "Return Point" Bookmark

Leave yourself a breadcrumb trail. At the end of each session, jot down what you were working on and what comes next. That way, when you return, you don't have to start over.

### The 3-Project Rule

Too many open projects = scattered focus. Try this: One main project, one "light" side project, and one fun/experimental piece. That's your limit.

### Weekly Check-In

Every Sunday, glance over your writing week. Ask: What did I touch? What got lost? What do I want to return to first?

### The Visual Anchor

Post a visual prompt where you write: a cover mockup, character photo, quote, or scene map. It gives your brain a clear "entry point."

### The 15-Minute Tidy

Once a week, take 15 minutes to clean up your digital or physical writing space. Just enough to keep chaos manageable.

### The Just-One-Thing List

Instead of long to-do lists, keep a sticky note with your next most important task. When it's done, make a new one.

### DIY Writing Dashboard

Create a super simple tracker—physical or digital—with columns like: Project, Next Step, Status, Notes.

### Your Turn!

## CHOOSE TWO TOOLS

After reviewing the toolkit, pick two strategies that feel most helpful for you right now. For each one, write a small, clear action step you'll take to practice it this week.

*Examples:*
- If you choose the **Return Point Bookmark,** your action step might be: "Before closing my doc today, I'll write a note to future me about what's next."
- If you choose the **Weekly Check-in,** your action step might by: "Set up a time on Sunday when I can review my week and update my organization tools."
- If you choose the **DIY Writing Dashboard,** your action step might be: "Sketch a simple 3-column list in my notebook tonight: Scene | Status | Notes."

## MY TOOLS AND ACTION STEPS

Tool #1 I'm Choosing:

_____

Action Step I'll Take:

_____

Tool #2 I'm Choosing:

_____

Action Step I'll Take:

_____

## THE DISORGANIZED'S GUIDEPOST

You need a gentle guidepost that keeps you connected to your story, even when life gets messy. This is a simple phrase you can return to when you're scattered or spinning. Here are some examples:

- "Start with what's in front of me."
- "One task, one session, one win."
- "Chaos doesn't stop me. Curiosity moves me."

**My guidepost phrase:**

_____

# mapping your novel journey

**Just a few intentional moves forward . . .**

It's easy to get overwhelmed by all the "shoulds," unfinished pieces, and scattered notes. That's why this week's goal is simple: name just one small, meaningful step each day that helps you reconnect with your writing, and follow through. Start with 2–3 tiny steps that feel doable. Keep it easy and focused.

## QUICK IDEAS FOR SMALL STEPS

(Choose or modify!)

- Revisit one scene and write a note about what's missing.
- Organize your draft titles or chapters in a list.
- Add a bullet-point "what happens next" to your current page.
- Jot down a 3-step plan for finishing one open writing task.
- Spend 10 minutes cleaning up one messy folder or notebook.
- Label your scenes with sticky notes or emojis to track progress.
- Print or copy one inspiring quote to keep near your writing space.

## MY SMALL STEPS FOR THE WEEK

| Day | One small action... | Did I take it? |
|---|---|---|
| **Monday** | | |
| **Tuesday** | | |
| **Wednesday** | | |
| **Thursday** | | |
| **Friday** | | |
| **Saturday** | | |
| **Sunday** | | |

# NOVEL-WRITING ROADMAP

## Step 1: Capture, don't control.

- Open a notebook or doc and start listing every scene or idea you've written.
- Use sticky notes, index cards, or digital folders to group your thoughts.
- Don't worry about the order. Just get it out of your head and onto the page.

*Examples:*
- Create a new doc called "Story Fragments - Catch All." Copy every scene into it.
- Grab a stack of index cards and start transferring each idea, one per card.

**My non-controlling capture:**

_____

## Step 2: Shape the mess, lightly.

- Write a short summary of your story's arc (beginning, middle, end).
- List 3-5 key turning points without overthinking it.
- Use a whiteboard, wall, or document to keep it visible and editable.

*Examples:*
- "Act 1: She finds the journal • Act 2: It leads her to her birth mother • Act 3: She must choose truth or comfort"
- "Start in the market • Run-in with rival • Climactic choice at old house"

**My light outline:**

_____

## Step 3: Create a follow-through habit.

- Choose a consistent writing trigger—same time, place, or ritual.
- Pick one day a week as your non-negotiable writing session.
- End each writing session by jotting down where to pick up next time.

*Examples:*
- "After I make coffee, I write until the timer goes off."
- "I'll stop mid-sentence so it's easy to start tomorrow."

**My follow-through routine:**

_____

# carry your structure forward

**The more scattered you feel, the more powerful a little structure can become.**

When you're used to writing in chaotic bursts—or not writing at all—it's easy to believe that you're just "not the type to be consistent." But consistency is about creating flexible patterns that work with your brain, not against it. You don't have to become a perfectly organized person. Below are some common Disorganized thoughts and how you might start shifting them toward support and clarity.

## SHIFT YOUR SELF-TALK

| Disorganized Thought | Structure Reframe |
|---|---|
| "I have too many ideas to pick just 1." | "I can start with one to see where it leads." |
| "I always lose track of where I was." | "I can leave myself a breadcrumb to return to next time." |
| "I've tried organizational apps, calendars, & lists." | "I can keep looking for the system that works." |
| "I keep losing track. I should just quit." | "I'm building a rhythm that works for me." |

### Your Turn
Write down a Disorganized thought and answer with a new structure-oriented voice.

| Disorganized Thought | Structure Reframe |
|---|---|
|  |  |
|  |  |
|  |  |
|  |  |

## YOUR STRUCTURE-INSPIRED PLAN

**1. What's one thing I'll say to myself the next time I feel too scattered to write?**
(Example: "I don't need the perfect plan. I just need a place to begin.")

_____

**2. What's one anchor or habit I can create to help me stay on track?**
(Example: Leave a note about what to write next. Open the same playlist each time.)

_____

**3. What's one way I'll reward myself for following through, even just a little?**
(Example: A sticker, a colored checkmark, a post in my writer group.)

_____

## LOOKING BACK

Every time you choose one thing over everything, you strengthen your creative focus. Over time, you can create a rhythm that honors both your mind and your mission. And now you have something new:

- Awareness of your patterns.
- Gentle structures to reduce chaos.
- New tools for clarity and follow-through.
- A writing rhythm that matches how you work.

# structure commitment

*I commit to creating a structure that works for me, even if it looks different from anyone else's."*

Signed: _____

Date: _____

# meet the overthinker

**You want to write, but you keep thinking. And thinking. And thinking.**

One idea leads to another, then to three more, then to a full spiral of what-ifs and not-quites and "maybe this instead." You tell yourself you're just being thorough. But the truth is, you're stuck in your head, while your words are waiting for you to climb out.

As an Overthinker, your procrastination often stems from a fear of making the wrong choice. You delay starting your novel because you're not sure which idea is best. You over-outline or endlessly revise, hoping to protect yourself from mistakes. But instead of writing, you end up mentally circling your story until your momentum fades.

It's not that you don't want to move forward. You just want to be certain of your choices before you do. The problem? Certainty never arrives. In this section, you'll learn how to pause the overthinking loop and rediscover what it feels like to make meaningful progress.

## COMMON TRAITS OF AN OVERTHINKER WRITER

- Delay choosing a story idea or direction for fear of picking the wrong one.
- Over-prepare, research excessively, or build overly complex outlines.
- Constantly revise instead of drafting new material.
- Obsess over small details like character names, word choice, sentence rhythm.
- Ruminate over feedback or worry endlessly about what others will think.
- Second-guess nearly every writing decision.
- Struggle to trust your own creative instincts.

## SELF-CHECK: DO YOU RECOGNIZE THIS PATTERN?

Check all that apply:
- ☐ I struggle to decide which idea to work on because I want to choose the best one.
- ☐ I tend to plan, research, or analyze more than I write.
- ☐ I revise the same scenes multiple times instead of finishing my draft.
- ☐ I feel anxious about writing something that might later turn out "wrong."
- ☐ I often feel overwhelmed by all the possible directions my story could go.
- ☐ I seek out feedback but then overanalyze what it means.
- ☐ I wait to write until I feel fully prepared, but I never quite do.

# the out-of-the-loop matrix

When you're stuck in overthinking, even simple writing tasks can feel like solving a puzzle with no edges. This matrix gives you a fast way out. Instead of spiraling in thought, pick the moment that sounds most like you in the moment and take the tiny action beside it. Each small act interrupts the paralysis loop.

| When I catch myself... | Then I will... |
|---|---|
| Obsessing over "the right way" to start | Set a 10-minute timer and begin writing any part, even if it's out of order. |
| Thinking through every option before choosing | Pick one draft direction and label it "Version A" to reduce pressure. |
| Delaying until I feel more certain | Write a list of 3 next steps and choose one to do. |
| Questioning whether my idea is good enough | Freewrite for 5 minutes about why I care about this idea. |
| Analyzing every sentence | Draft a paragraph without stopping. |
| Rethinking yesterday's work instead of writing new words | Pause research, highlight open questions, and draft around them. |
| Researching "just a little more" before writing | Decide to write for only five minutes before switching to research. Keep writing if you want! |

**JOURNAL PROMPT**

Where does overthinking tend to derail your writing most? Is it when you're deciding what to write, trying to fix a scene, or choosing between options?

# shift your writing mindset

**You don't need perfect clarity to begin. Action shapes the path ahead.**

Your mind is constantly trying to "figure it all out" before you take the next step. You might tell yourself that once you've considered every angle, then you'll be ready to write. But clarity doesn't come from thinking alone. It comes from *doing—moving through* the uncertainty instead of avoiding it. You don't have to stop overthinking overnight, but you can gently retrain your mind to prioritize movement over mental loops.

## MINDSET REFRAME #1

**Old mindset:** "If I think long enough, I'll figure it out perfectly."
**New mindset:** "Clarity comes through action, not before it."
Overthinking promises safety, but often delivers paralysis instead. You can't solve your creative problems in theory alone. Even a "wrong" move gives you new information. Once you're in motion, the path ahead sharpens, and choices get easier.

**Reflect:**
When was a time you thought about a project for so long that it stopped feeling exciting?

_____

What happened when you finally took action, or what might have happened if you had?

_____

## MINDSET REFRAME #2

**Old mindset:** "If I don't choose the best path, I'll waste time or mess it up."
**New mindset:** "Every step teaches me something I couldn't learn by waiting."
There's no perfect choice. Every draft, paragraph, and creative detour adds to your experience. Even if you pivot later, that's not failure—it's progress with direction. The only way to waste time is to stay frozen.

**Reflect:**
Think of a moment when indecision held you back. What did it cost you?

_____

What's one "imperfect" action you're willing to try this week, just to gather creative data?

_____

**QUICK ACTION**

List two small ways you'll remind yourself of these new mindsets this week (i.e., sticky note, background on your writing device, voice memo, visual cue):

_____

_____

# your personal mindset reframe

Shifting your mindset is about interrupting the pattern with a truth that helps you move forward rather than staying stuck. In the space below, create your own personalized reframe. This will be your anchor—a thought strong enough to challenge the thinking logic and help you choose motion over mental traffic jams.

## STEP 1: RECOGNIZE THE PATTERN

What's a common thought you have that keeps you spinning in indecision?
(Example: "I have to make the perfect choice before I start.")

_____

_____

## STEP 2: WRITE A MORE SUPPORTIVE TRUTH

What new thought will you practice this week that allows for progress and learning?
(Example: "I can choose one path and see where it leads. I can always adjust.")

_____

_____

**MY LOOP-BREAKER MINDSET CARD**

Use an index card, sticky note, or whatever you like. Write it big, decorate it, or make a small "badge" for your writing space.

**Old thought I'm replacing:** _____

**New thought I'm practicing:** _____

# my hidden rewards

**Overthinking feels productive, but often delays the real work.**

For you, procrastination can look deceptively like progress. You're brainstorming, planning, and revising your outline again, so it feels like you're working. But if you're not actually moving forward with your draft, your brain might be clinging to certain hidden rewards. These are signs your mind is trying to avoid discomfort, uncertainty, or decision fatigue. The problem? These short-term payoffs often cost you long-term momentum, confidence, and growth. Let's name them so you can decide if they're worth what they're taking from you.

## WHAT ARE YOUR HIDDEN REWARDS?

**When I avoid writing by overthinking, I might be getting:** (check all that apply)

☐ The illusion of progress without the risk of failure.

☐ A sense of control by keeping everything in my head.

☐ Protection from choosing the "wrong" creative path.

☐ Relief from the pressure of making a decision.

☐ A way to postpone vulnerability or judgment.

☐ Avoidance of imperfect or messy work.

☐ The comfort of staying in the idea phase, where everything still feels possible.

Other hidden payoffs I've noticed:

_____

_____

_____

_____

**JOURNAL PROMPT**

What have these hidden rewards been costing you creatively, emotionally, or personally? (Think about lost time, abandoned projects, mental fatigue, or the feeling of always circling but never landing.)

# future payoffs

Now imagine that in the coming weeks and months, you start acting despite the urge to keep analyzing. You start unlocking new kinds of creative energy. What might you gain from that sort of approach? (Check all that apply.)

**If I take action, even without feeling certain, I could gain:**

☐ Real movement on the stories I care about.
☐ Confidence in my ability to choose and adjust.
☐ Relief from constant mental looping.
☐ More finished projects and fewer abandoned ones.
☐ A stronger trust in my creative instincts.
☐ The joy of discovering what works while writing.
☐ Greater creative freedom by letting go of "perfect."

### OTHER BENEFITS I WANT TO CLAIM

_____     _____

_____     _____

### DESIGN YOUR "CHOOSE-AND-MOVE" CARD

You hesitate to move forward because you're trying to make the best decision or avoid the wrong one. This card helps you cut through the swirl of overanalysis and return to forward action. In the space below, create your own "Choose-and-Move" Card. Use power phrases, reminders, or visual cues that help you stop spinning and start doing. Keep it somewhere you'll see it during writing sessions to interrupt the loop.

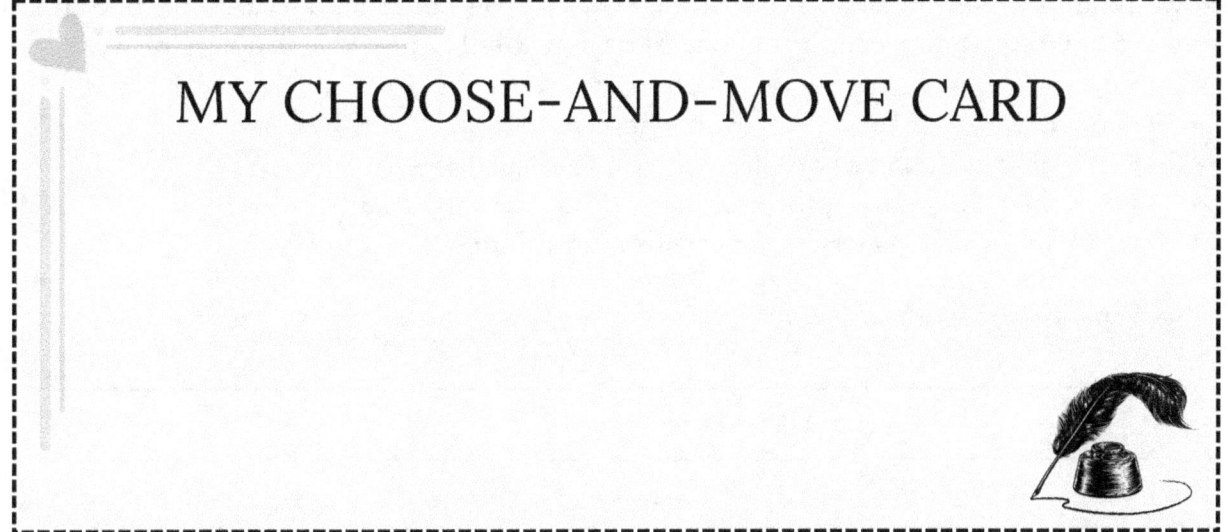

MY CHOOSE-AND-MOVE CARD

# your new writer identity

**You main goal is to create trust in your creative instincts.**

When you see yourself as someone who's "always overthinking," you start to build an identity around that belief. You hesitate, second-guess, and stall out because that's who you've come to expect yourself to be. But your identity isn't fixed. It's shaped by small, repeatable actions. And with every choice to move forward, even when you don't have all the answers, you start becoming someone new: a writer who chooses, creates, and adjusts as they go.

## MY WRITING IDENTITY SHIFT

### Step 1: How do you see yourself now?
Let's get honest. What labels or beliefs do you often repeat to yourself when you're stuck in overthinking? Here are some common Overthinker identity thoughts:

- "I can't move forward until I figure it all out."
- "If I make the wrong choice, I'll ruin everything."
- "I get stuck in my head and never reach the page."
- "I revise endlessly because nothing feels good enough."

Now, write 3 beliefs, labels, or self-messages you often carry about yourself as a writer.

_____

_____

_____

### Step 2: Who do you want to become?
Now imagine yourself six months from now. You've practiced choosing and moving forward without waiting for perfection. What new identity are you stepping into?

- "I'm a writer who takes action even when I'm unsure."
- "I make creative choices and trust myself to adjust later."
- "I finish things because I stop waiting for the perfect version."
- "I let writing show me what works instead of figuring it all out first."

Write 3 beliefs you want to grow into.

_____

_____

_____

**Step 3: What would that version of you do next?**
Next, using the ideas you wrote down, you'll create a simple statement that captures who you are becoming as a writer.

Try this formula:
**Even though I usually _____, I'm learning to _____.**

Here are some examples:
- "Even though I usually rethink every step, I'm learning to write first and decide later."
- "Even though I usually stall when I'm unsure, I'm learning to choose one direction and move."
- "Even though I usually delay for too long, I'm learning to create progress by taking action."

## MY IDENTITY BRIDGE STATEMENT

_____

_____

_____

## ENCOURAGE YOURSELF!

**Remember:** Every time you take action, you build trust in your ability to move forward. You gradually start to see that you don't need to solve everything before you begin. You can interrupt the spiral, choose one clear step, and let progress quiet the noise.

> ## I'm learning to move before I have it all figured out.

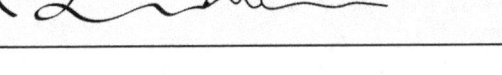

# tools to write past overthinking

**The moment you take action, your brain quiets down.**

Overthinking feeds on delay. It loves when you circle the same question without resolution! But once your fingers move across the page, something shifts. The mental noise softens, decisions start to feel less final, and writing becomes possible again. The tools on this page help you get to that moment faster, where thought gives way to motion and the work finally begins.

These aren't meant to make you stop thinking altogether. They're here to give your brain a path to follow, so your energy shifts from looping to momentum.

## TOOLKIT FOR THE OVERDOER

### Use a "Pick One" Prompt Jar

Write 10–20 creative choices (scenes, questions, ideas) on slips of paper. When you get stuck, draw one and go with it for 15 minutes.

### Set a "Messy Draft" Timer

Give yourself 10 minutes to write the next scene without stopping, deleting, or rereading. Tell yourself, "This version doesn't have to be the only one. I can adjust later."

### Use a Placeholder Habit

When you get stuck in uncertainty (e.g., names, facts, descriptions), drop a [placeholder] and keep moving. Return later. This breaks the perfection loop.

### Limit Re-Thinking Time

If you find yourself reconsidering a past section, set a 5-minute timer: reread, jot notes, and move forward. You don't need to fix it before drafting more.

### "First Choice, Fast Draft" Rule

When given two or more options, pick one and move forward for at least 500 words. Train your brain to make a call and explore it, not endlessly debate.

### Anchor with a Mantra

Use short phrases like: "Choose and go." "Done is data." "Forward, not loopy!" Say it aloud or write it at the top of your document.

### Work in Constrained Containers

Instead of sprawling writing sessions, limit yourself to one focused task in one sitting: "Write one scene," "Answer one question," or "Sketch one moment."

### Your Turn!

## CHOOSE TWO TOOLS

After reviewing the toolkit, pick two strategies that feel most helpful for you right now. For each one, write a small, clear action step you'll take to practice it this week.

*Examples:*
- If you choose the **Pick One Prompt Jar** tool, your action step might be: "Write 10 creative prompts on index cards and draw one before my next session."
- If you choose the **Placeholder Habit** tool, your action step might be: "Use [fill this in later] during my next session so I don't stop drafting to solve everything."
- If you choose the **First Choice, Fast Draft** rule, your action step might be: "Choose one story path today and write 300 words in that direction without backtracking."

## MY TOOLS AND ACTION STEPS

Tool #1 I'm Choosing:

_____

Action Step I'll Take:

_____

Tool #2 I'm Choosing:

_____

Action Step I'll Take:

_____

## THE OVERTHINKER'S DISRUPTION PHRASE

You need a simple cue to break the loop—a phrase that cuts through the swirl of indecision and reminds you that action is what clarifies the path. Write a personal mantra or anchor phrase you can use when your thoughts start circling. Examples:

- "Thinking more won't make it easier. Writing will."
- "Decide, draft, adjust later."
- "Let the words lead the way."

**My disruption phrase:**

_____

# mapping your novel journey

**Small choices get you writing instead of thinking.**

Overthinking loves a big, open-ended project. It gives your brain endless angles to spin. But tiny, focused actions shrink the mental clutter. This week, commit to three low-pressure steps you can actually complete. Each time you follow through, you teach your mind: I can choose, and I can move.

## QUICK IDEAS FOR SMALL STEPS

(Choose or modify!)

- Draft one scene, even if it feels like the "wrong" one.
- Jot down 3 possible directions for a stuck moment and pick one.
- Write a placeholder for a section you're unsure about.
- Set a 10-minute timer and write, no matter how messy.
- Choose one plot hole and sketch a possible fix.
- Finish a paragraph without rereading it.
- Decide on a title or character name that will work just for now.

## MY SMALL STEPS FOR THE WEEK

| Day | One small action... | Did I take it? |
|---|---|---|
| Monday | | |
| Tuesday | | |
| Wednesday | | |
| Thursday | | |
| Friday | | |
| Saturday | | |
| Sunday | | |

## NOVEL-WRITING ROADMAP

### Step 1: Shrink the field of options.

- Skip the big picture. Instead, start with one scene you feel curious about.
- Use a timer to make a decision quickly (Example: "I'll pick a POV in 60 seconds").
- Limit idea bouncing. Choose one draft direction and explore it for 500 words.

*Examples:*
- "I'll write the moment my character makes a mistake they regret."
- "I'll try this scene in first person, just to see how it feels."

**My narrowed option:**

_____

### Step 2: Create a lightweight outline.

- Write a one-sentence version of your story.
- Expand into 5 key turning points.
- Create a simple scene list—just a few steps ahead.

*Examples:*
- Key points: Girl finds artifact, gets in trouble, friend help, major loss, makes a choice
- Scene list: Exploring attic → Confrontation with brother → Memory flashback → Reveal at school → Midnight escape

**My lightweight outline:**

_____

### Step 3: Build a decision-friendly writing routine.

- Set two 15- to 30-minute writing blocks each week.
- Start sessions by picking one micro-goal (example: "Write a rough version of chapter 2").
- End each session with a short "next step" note for tomorrow. You'll thank yourself later.

*Examples:*
- "Write for 25 minutes on Tuesdays and Thursdays before lunch—no decisions allowed."
- "Light a candle, turn off Wi-Fi, and use a sticky note that says: DONE IS DATA."

**My decision-friendly routine:**

_____

# carry your movement forward

**Creation begins when you stop waiting for certainty and start moving anyway.**

Overthinking means your brain is working overtime to prevent regret, mistakes, or wasted effort. But staying mentally stuck costs you the chance to create something real. The key isn't to shut down your thoughts, but to stop waiting for the perfect ones before you act. Below are some common Overthinker thoughts and how you can shift them into more grounded, forward-moving beliefs.

## SHIFT YOUR SELF-TALK

| Overthinking Thought | Movement Reframe |
|---|---|
| "I should think this through more." | "A quick step forward will teach me more than circling it again." |
| "What if I pick the wrong direction?" | "Any direction gives me data. I can always adjust." |
| "I need to plan this better first." | "Planning helps, but doing reveals." |
| "I'm not ready to write yet." | "I'm ready enough to try." |

### Your Turn

Write down an Overthinking thought and answer with a new movement-oriented voice.

| Overthinking Thought | Movement Reframe |
|---|---|
|  |  |
|  |  |
|  |  |
|  |  |

## YOUR MOVEMENT-PROMOTING PLAN

**1. What's one reminder you'll use the next time your brain starts spinning in circles?**
(Example: "Pick something and go.")

_____

**2. What's one action that helps you feel less mentally tangled and more in motion?**
(Example: time-limited choices, rough drafting, moving your body before you begin.)

_____

**3. What's one way you'll celebrate any decision you follow through on?**
(Example: a sticker, a deep breath, a short reflection on what you learned.)

_____

## LOOKING BACK

Every time you interrupt an overthinking spiral and take action, you're building trust in your ability to choose. and that trust becomes your creative momentum. The old patterns may still show up. That's okay. Now you have something new:

- Awareness of when you're stuck in loops.
- Tools to help you move forward even in uncertainty.
- A new identity grounded in creative motion.
- Proof that your next step doesn't have to be perfect to be powerful.

## movement commitment

*I commit to choosing motion over mental loops. Even one small step forward matters.*

Signed: _____

Date: _____

# meet the tired

**You want to write, but when the time comes, you feel drained.**

Your brain fogs, your body slumps, and your motivation disappears. You tell yourself you'll write later, when you have more energy. But later rarely comes.

As a Tired procrastinator, your delays aren't driven by fear or perfectionism—they're rooted in low energy. Fatigue, burnout, chronic health issues, or a stressful, overloaded life can make writing feel like one more thing you just don't have the capacity for. The blank page becomes too heavy. So you scroll, snack, or nap instead, and then beat yourself up for not getting anything done.

This pattern can feel discouraging, but it doesn't mean you're doomed. Your brain and body are simply crying out for restoration. In this chapter, you'll learn how to manage your energy, reclaim your rhythm, and create a writing life that supports you, instead of draining you.

## COMMON TRAITS OF A TIRED WRITER

- Intend to write but feel too exhausted to follow through.
- Sit down to write but can't seem to focus or stay alert.
- Feel burned out by your day job, caregiving, or other life responsibilities.
- Push yourself until you crash, then avoid writing for days.
- Tell yourself you'll write when you have more energy (but that moment never comes).
- Feel guilty for not "doing enough," which drains your energy further.
- Love writing but rarely feel restored or excited by it anymore.

## SELF-CHECK: DO YOU RECOGNIZE THIS PATTERN?

Check all that apply:
- ☐ I often intend to write, but I feel too tired when the time comes.
- ☐ I experience bursts of energy, followed by long periods of avoidance.
- ☐ Even small writing tasks can feel overwhelming.
- ☐ I feel guilty when I procrastinate, which drains me further.
- ☐ I struggle to concentrate or stay on task while writing.
- ☐ I avoid writing because I know I'm too tired to do it well.
- ☐ I push through exhaustion, then crash hard and lose momentum.

# the renewal matrix

When your energy dips and your writing feels impossible, come back to this matrix. Each row shows a common Tired pattern and a small action that gently recharges your momentum. Just pick the one that fits your current mood and try the paired micro-move. It will help you make progress, even if it's small.

| When I catch myself... | Then I will... |
|---|---|
| Too tired to start | Set a 5-minute timer and open my draft. |
| Feeling foggy | Do 10 jumping jacks, listen to upbeat music, or stretch for 2 minutes. |
| Wanting to write but too drained | Record a voice memo of ideas while lying down. |
| Feeling guilty for resting | Write one kind sentence to myself to spark writing. |
| Sitting at the desk but zoning out | Try writing while standing or walking. |
| Too tired to think | Copy a favorite passage from a book I love. |
| Can't focus for long | Try a 10/5 cycle: 10 minutes writing, 5 minutes break. |

**JOURNAL PROMPT**

What does your tiredness usually look like? Is it physical, mental, emotional, or all three? What patterns do you notice around the times you skip writing?

# shift your writing mindset

**Writing can restore you, not just drain you.**

It's easy to believe you have to wait for energy to return before you can be productive again. But writing doesn't have to be a high-energy task. It can be something that grounds you, restores you, or even soothes your system if you learn to approach it with care. The more you practice writing in gentle, energy-mindful ways, the more you build a sustainable rhythm. Below are two key mindset shifts that can help you write from a place of restoration, not exhaustion.

## MINDSET REFRAME #1

**Old mindset:** "I'm too tired to write. I'll do it when I have more energy."
**New mindset:** "I can write gently, even when I'm tired."
Sometimes showing up in a softer way—writing from the couch, jotting a few lines, or speaking thoughts into your phone—is more than enough. Writing isn't always about force. It can also be about quiet connection with the page.

**Reflect:**
When have you written something valuable while feeling low energy or not fully "on"?

_____

What helped you do it?

_____

## MINDSET REFRAME #2

**Old mindset:** "If I can't give it my full energy, it's not worth doing."
**New mindset:** "Small, low-effort progress still counts, and helps me build momentum."
A few gentle steps, such as scrawled notes, a soft edit, or a single sentence, can spark more than you think. And even when they don't? They're still a win. You showed up for your writing life in a way that honors your real life.

**Reflect:**
What's one tiny way you can lower the pressure around writing this week?

_____

How might that ignite your energy rather than depleting it?

_____

**QUICK ACTION**

List two small ways you'll remind yourself of these new mindsets this week (i.e. sticky note, background on your writing device, voice memo, visual cue):

_____

_____

# your personal mindset reframe

You need to approach writing in a way that restores rather than depletes. The trick is learning how to work with your energy instead of against it. The card below is your personal cue to shift from guilt and fatigue into soft creative motion. Let it help you rekindle your spark, one gentle step at a time.

## STEP 1: RECOGNIZE THE PATTERN

What's a draining thought you often have when you're too tired to write?
(Example: "I'm too exhausted to create anything meaningful.")

_____

_____

## STEP 2: WRITE A MORE SUPPORTIVE TRUTH

What's a more compassionate, energy-aware truth you want to practice instead?
(Example: "Even one quiet sentence can reconnect me to my voice.")

_____

_____

**MY STEADY-SPARK MINDSET CARD**

Use an index card, sticky note, or whatever you like. Write it big, decorate it, or make a small "badge" for your writing space.

**Old thought I'm replacing:** _____

**New thought I'm practicing:** _____

# my hidden rewards

**Procrastination feels like protection, especially when you're exhausted.**

As a Tired writer, your delays often come from real fatigue. Skipping writing can feel like a form of self-care in the moment. And sometimes, it is. But when procrastination becomes your default response, it may be offering short-term comfort at the expense of long-term creative fulfillment.

The key is to notice what you're getting from the delay, and then decide if it's truly helping you feel restored, or keeping you disconnected from what you love.

## WHAT ARE YOUR HIDDEN REWARDS?

**When I avoid writing, I might be getting:** (check all that apply)

- ☐ A break from pressure or high expectations.
- ☐ Temporary relief from mental fatigue.
- ☐ Avoidance of the "energy crash" that follows pushing too hard.
- ☐ The comfort of rest (even if it doesn't always feel restorative).
- ☐ Protection from the fear that I won't do my best work when tired.
- ☐ An excuse to disconnect from the guilt of not being productive.
- ☐ A pause that feels safer than confronting how drained I really am.

Other hidden payoffs I've noticed:

_____

_____

_____

_____

**JOURNAL PROMPT**

What do these hidden rewards cost you over time emotionally, creatively, or personally? (Think about projects delayed, the joy of writing lost, or the tension between rest and guilt.)

# future payoffs

Now imagine that in the coming weeks and months, you let go of the pressure to be high-performing and instead focus on small, doable steps. You reconnect with the part of writing that fills you up. What might you gain from that approach? (Check all that apply.)

**If I take action, even without 100% energy, I could gain:**

☐ A writing practice that supports me instead of draining me.
☐ Confidence that I can create even on low-energy days.
☐ Freedom from guilt and shame cycles.
☐ A deeper connection to my voice through softness, not force.
☐ Permission to write without overexertion.
☐ A greater sense of calm and presence when I create.
☐ Real progress over time, built from small, steady actions.

## OTHER BENEFITS I WANT TO CLAIM

_____     _____

_____     _____

## DESIGN YOUR "WHY-IT'S-WORTH-IT" CARD

When you're tired, it's easy to forget what writing gives back to you. This card is your reminder that even when your energy is low, your writing still matters. In the space below, write or design your own "Why It's Worth It" Card. Use single words, phrases, images, or doodles—whatever feels natural. Keep it where it can gently remind you to show up!

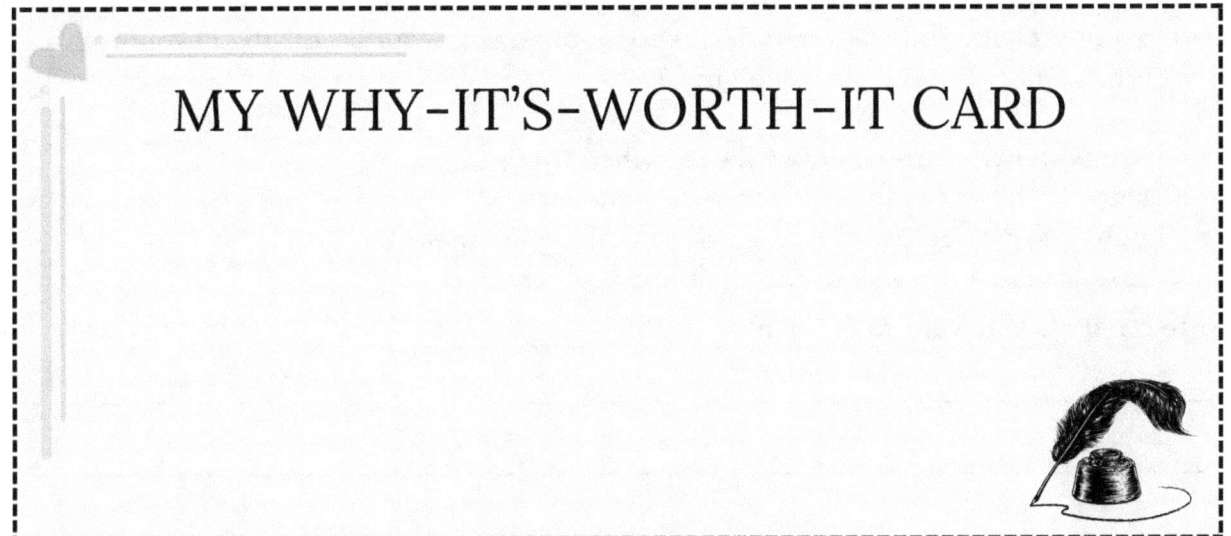

MY WHY-IT'S-WORTH-IT CARD

# your new writer identity

**Believe that slow, gentle progress is still valid.**

When you think of yourself as "someone who never has enough energy to write," you reinforce that identity every time you skip the page out of exhaustion. Your actions, thoughts, and emotions begin to orbit that belief. Overcoming this self-concept means shifting how you see yourself: from "I'm someone who's always too drained to write" to "I'm someone who shows up in a way that honors my energy." Gradually, you become someone who makes regular progress, even if it's slow.

## MY WRITING IDENTITY SHIFT

### Step 1: How do you see yourself now?
Let's get honest: What identity messages have formed around your energy, motivation, or consistency? Here are some common Tired identity thoughts:

- "I want to write, but I'm always too tired."
- "If I don't feel fully rested, it's not even worth trying."
- "I lose steam after just a few days of trying."
- "I'll never be consistent because my energy always runs out."

Now, write 3 beliefs, labels, or self-messages you often carry about yourself as a writer.

_____

_____

_____

### Step 2: Who do you want to become?
Now imagine yourself six months from now. You've been writing in ways that support your energy, not drain it. And you've started reconnecting with your creativity on your terms. What new identity are you stepping into?

- "I'm a writer who creates gently, even when I'm tired."
- "I show up for my writing with care, not pressure."
- "I don't need to be at 100% to make something meaningful."
- "I take small creative steps that help me feel restored."

Write 3 beliefs you want to grow into.

_____

_____

_____

**Step 3: What would that version of you do next?**
Next, using the ideas you wrote down, create a simple statement that captures who you are becoming as a writer.

Try this formula:
**Even though I usually** _____**, I'm learning to** _____**.**

Here are some examples:
- "Even though I usually skip writing when I'm drained, I'm learning to create soft moments that don't cost me energy."
- "Even though I usually wait for the perfect time, I'm learning to write in small, supportive ways."
- "Even though I usually feel too tired to begin, I'm learning that even one gentle page counts."

## MY IDENTITY BRIDGE STATEMENT

_____

_____

_____

## ENCOURAGE YOURSELF!

**Remember:** Every small choice you make—to open your document, write a soft sentence, or return after a low-energy day—is a quiet act of devotion to your creative self. You may not have many days where you feel fully energized. That's okay. You just have to keep showing up in whatever way you can in the moment.

> ## Even when I'm too tired to do it all, I can still do something that matters.

# tools to write through tiredness

**Use tools that help you get the most out of the energy you have.**

Tiredness drains your motivation, focus, and belief that writing is possible. But you don't need to wait until you feel energized to begin. The right tools can help you write in a way that restores you, not exhausts you further.

Think of these tools like cozy supports—gentle structures that help you stay connected to your creativity, even on your lowest days. Some will work better than others, and that's okay. Your job isn't to do them all. It's to experiment and discover what helps you write without pushing past your limits.

## TOOLKIT FOR THE TIRED

### Set a 5-Minute "Soft Start" Timer

When you feel too tired to begin, set a timer for just 5 minutes. Open your document and sit with it—no pressure to write. Just be with your words.

### Use Voice Notes Instead of Typing

Speak your ideas aloud while walking, resting, or lying down. This lowers the energy barrier and keeps ideas flowing when you don't feel up to writing.

### Create a Low-Energy Writing Nest

Make a comfy, cozy space for writing. Think blanket, tea, soft lighting, and zero pressure. Your body needs to feel safe and relaxed.

### "One Sentence, Then Decide" Rule

Commit to writing just one sentence. After that, decide if you want to keep going. Often, the first line is all it takes to get started.

### Keep a "Rest-and-Write" Rotation

Alternate short writing bursts with real rest. Try 10 minutes writing, 10 minutes lying down with no phone. Let the rhythm restore you.

### Track Energy, Not Word Count

Instead of measuring output, track how writing made you feel. Did it soothe you? Energize you? Even soft engagement is a win.

### Pick a Soothing Ritual to Begin

Light a candle. Play soft music. Hold a warm mug. Use a familiar signal to ease yourself gently into writing time.

### Your Turn!

## CHOOSE TWO TOOLS

After reviewing the toolkit, pick two strategies that feel most helpful for you right now. For each one, write a small, clear action step you'll take to practice it this week.

*Examples:*
- If you choose the **Soft Start Timer** tool, your action step would be: "Set a 5-minute timer tomorrow and open your draft—no pressure to write."
- If you choose the **Voice Notes** tool, your action step might be: "Record a 2-minute idea while walking or resting today."
- If you choose the **Writing Nest** tool, your action step could be: "Gather your blanket, candle, and tea and write from the couch this weekend."

## MY TOOLS AND ACTION STEPS

Tool #1 I'm Choosing:

_____

Action Step I'll Take:

_____

Tool #2 I'm Choosing:

_____

Action Step I'll Take:

_____

## THE TIRED'S INVITING PHRASE

You need a simple phrase can serve as your invitation back to the page, even when you're not feeling up to it. Write a personal mantra or anchor phrase you can use when your energy is flagging. Examples:

- "One soft word is enough."
- "Tired is still allowed to create."
- "Resting and writing can coexist."

**My inviting phrase:**

_____

# mapping your novel journey

**Small steps protect your energy while reconnecting you to your words.**

When you're running low, even simple tasks can feel enormous. But tiny, intentional actions can slowly rebuild your rhythm without demanding more than you can give. This week, commit to three low-pressure, energy-aware steps that help you stay connected to your work.

## QUICK IDEAS FOR SMALL STEPS

(Choose or modify!)

- Record a voice memo of a scene idea while lying down.
- Write one sentence while sipping tea or coffee.
- Copy a favorite line from a book and reflect on it.
- Edit 1 paragraph with no pressure to improve it—just revisit it.
- Read an old piece you wrote and underline what still feels good.
- Write a short note to a character, even if it never makes it into the story.
- Spend 5 minutes imagining a setting, with no need to write it down.

## MY SMALL STEPS FOR THE WEEK

| Day | One small action... | Did I take it? |
|---|---|---|
| Monday | | |
| Tuesday | | |
| Wednesday | | |
| Thursday | | |
| Friday | | |
| Saturday | | |
| Sunday | | |

## NOVEL-WRITING ROADMAP

### Step 1: Make writing feel doable.

- Write in short bursts—5 to 15 minutes.
- Choose one part of your novel that feels easy or interesting right now.
- Use cozy tools like dictation, bullet points, sentence fragments.

*Examples:*
- "I'll record myself describing my setting while lying on the couch."
- "I'll rewrite a small scene I already like just to enjoy being with the story."

### My doable option:

_____

### Step 2: Outline in gentle layers.

- Write a one-sentence story idea.
- Jot 3 to 5 story beats—just enough to hold the shape.
- Sketch possible scenes in short phrases.

*Examples:*
- Key beats: Exile ➤ Reunion ➤ Revelation ➤ Choice ➤ Return
- Scene list: Forest camp ➤ Letter from home ➤ Confrontation ➤ Cliffside decision

### My layered outline:

_____

### Step 3: Create a sustainable writing rhythm.

- Choose 2-3 soft writing sessions per week (even 10-20 minutes).
- Tie writing to a gentle ritual (tea, blanket, music, warm-up journaling).
- Let "writing" include planning, thinking, revising, even dreaming.

*Examples:*
- "Every Monday and Thursday evening, I light a candle and write for 15 minutes."
- "On Saturday mornings, I take a walk and record a voice memo of story ideas."

### My sustainable writing rhythm:

_____

# carry your nourishment forward

**You can move forward without forcing your energy to keep up.**

Writing doesn't have to become another demand on your already overextended system. It can become a space where energy gently returns. With time, you can learn how to care for your creativity without burning yourself out. Below are some common thoughts Tired writers experience, and ways to reframe them into softer, kinder truths that help you keep writing.

## SHIFT YOUR SELF-TALK

| Tired Thought | Nourishing Reframe |
|---|---|
| "I'm too tired to write anything good." | "I will write without judging the result." |
| "If I'm not at 100%, what's the point?" | "What I can give today is enough." |
| "I'll write when I'm rested." | "Even quiet writing moments help me feel motivated." |
| "I can't stay consistent." | "I'm learning a rhythm that respects my energy." |

**Your Turn**

Write down a Tired thought and answer with a new nourishing voice.

| Tired Thought | Nourishing Reframe |
|---|---|
|  |  |
|  |  |
|  |  |
|  |  |

## YOUR NOURISHING PLAN

**1. What's one reminder you'll use when you're tempted to skip writing?**
(Examples: "Even ten minutes counts." "I don't need energy to begin—just willingness.")

_____

**2. What's one writing ritual that makes you feel supported rather than drained?**
(Examples: Writing in bed with a cup of tea; setting a 15-minute timer.)

_____

**3. What's one thing you'll stop doing to protect your energy?**
(Examples: Beating myself up for slow days; writing late at night when I know I need sleep.)

_____

## LOOKING BACK

Every time you choose to write with care instead of pressure, you're building trust in your ability to create sustainably, and that trust can become your creative foundation. The fatigue may still show up and the brain fog roll in, but that's okay. Now you have something new:

- Awareness of when you're pushing past your limits.
- Tools to support your creativity without draining it.
- A new identity grounded in self-compassion and rhythm.
- Proof that small, restful steps can still move your writing forward.

# nourishing commitment

### *I commit to writing in ways that nourish me. Even when I move slowly, I'm growing as a writer.*

Signed: _____

Date: _____

# meet the defier

**You want to write, but you will not bow to anyone else's ideas!**

As a Defier writer, you don't procrastinate out of fear or fatigue. For you, it's an act of resistance. Whether it's a deadline, a critique, or even your own schedule, you instinctively push back the moment something starts to feel like an obligation.

You value creative freedom more than almost anything. And when that freedom feels threatened, your inner rebel flares to life. Sometimes that means delaying projects, missing deadlines, or abandoning outlines entirely. Other times, it's subtle: nodding at feedback you'll never use or refusing to follow a "conventional" process because it just doesn't feel like you.

Unfortunately, when you get caught up in trying so hard to protect your freedom, you may be giving up your ability to progress with your writing. In this chapter, you'll find ways to keep your independence without slowing yourself down.

## COMMON TRAITS OF A DEFIER WRITER

- Bristle at writing advice or feedback, even when you asked for it.
- Lose motivation the moment a project becomes a "should."
- Procrastinate more when someone expects something from you.
- Dislike rigid writing goals, word counts, or deadlines.
- Feel like writing routines kill your creativity.
- Avoid revising because you fear losing control of your work.
- Push back, sometimes silently, against anyone who tells you what to do.

## SELF-CHECK: DO YOU RECOGNIZE THIS PATTERN?

Check all that apply:
- ☐ I procrastinate more when someone expects me to write.
- ☐ I resist writing routines, even ones I created myself.
- ☐ I feel stifled by outlines, word counts, or detailed plans.
- ☐ I avoid revising when I think it might change my original vision.
- ☐ I lose interest in projects that feel like obligations.
- ☐ I feel more motivated when no one's watching.
- ☐ I push back against rules, writing advice, or external pressure.

# the take-control matrix

When you're stuck in resistance mode, you need options for how to regain your feeling of freedom. This matrix gives you small, defiance-friendly actions that honor your independence while still getting words on the page. Each row pairs a common rebellious thought with a move that helps you take back creative control.

| When I think this... | Then I will... |
|---|---|
| "I don't want to do this right now." | Do a 5-minute "I'll just start" session to prove I choose the pace. |
| "Don't tell me how to write." | Break one writing rule on purpose. |
| "Deadlines kill my creativity." | Set a flexible goal that I define. |
| "Outlines are cages." | Sketch 3 rough scene ideas in any order—no structure required. |
| "I hate this stupid task." | Give myself 10 minutes to get into it. |
| "This feedback ruins my work." | Choose one note to ignore and one I want to explore. |
| "I'm not doing this just because I should." | Reconnect with why I care about this project in the first place. |

**JOURNAL PROMPT**

Where do you feel the most resistance in your writing life right now, and what (or who) do you feel it's directed toward?

# shift your writing mindset

**You don't have to obey the rules, but you do need to own your process.**

As a Defier, your resistance means you deeply value freedom, voice, and autonomy. But if you're not careful, that resistance can become your default setting, stalling projects that actually matter to you. You don't have to become a rule-follower. You just need to become the kind of writer who makes your own rules and then actually uses them to finish what you care about. Below are two powerful mindset shifts that can help you stop fighting your writing and start leading it.

## MINDSET REFRAME #1

**Old mindset:** "If someone expects this from me, I don't want to do it."
**New mindset:** "I get to define what matters and choose when and how to show up."
You're here to make something that's fully yours. That means stepping away from obligation, but not from ownership. Writing isn't something you owe someone. It's something you get to claim.

**Reflect:**
When has resistance pulled you off track from something you actually wanted to finish?

_____

What would it look like to reclaim it on your terms?

_____

## MINDSET REFRAME #2

**Old mindset:** "Routines, outlines, and deadlines kill my creativity."
**New mindset:** "I can create flexible structures that serve me, not control me."
You can build systems that feel like freedom instead of confinement. Think short sessions, soft deadlines, loose outlines, or creative rituals that *you* choose. The key is to exercise your right to choose more often, and in a way that supports your writing dreams.

**Reflect:**
What small structure could help you protect your creative independence without making you feel boxed in?

_____

When have you created something powerful by working in your own way?

_____

**QUICK ACTION**

List two small ways you'll remind yourself of these new mindsets this week (i.e., sticky note, background on your writing device, voice memo, visual cue):

_____

_____

# your personal mindset reframe

When resistance becomes your default, it can block the very thing you're trying to protect: your progress, your voice, and your power. The card below is your personal reminder that you're not being forced to do what you don't want to do. Instead of giving in to pressure, you can claim your own path.

## STEP 1: RECOGNIZE THE PATTERN

What's a rebellious or resistant thought that often shows up when you're avoiding writing? (Example: "I'm tired of being told what to do. I'll write when I feel like it.")

_____

_____

## STEP 2: WRITE A MORE EMPOWERING TRUTH

What's a more empowered truth that reminds you you're still in charge? (Example: "This story matters to me. I'm writing it because I choose to.")

_____

_____

## MY CREATIVE-OWNERSHIP CARD

Use an index card, sticky note, or whatever you like. Write it big, decorate it, or make a small "badge" for your writing space.

**Old thought I'm replacing:** _____

**New thought I'm practicing:** _____

# my hidden rewards

**Procrastination can feel powerful when it protects your independence.**

Procrastination often feels like resistance, but underneath it, there's usually a desire to reclaim control. Delaying that draft, skipping the outline, or ignoring advice can feel like protecting your independence in a world full of expectations. There's power in saying, "I'll do it my way." To move forward, it helps to name what you've been getting out of procrastination. It might be space, autonomy, relief from pressure, or something else. Once you know what you've been protecting, you can find healthier ways to honor it.

## WHAT ARE YOUR HIDDEN REWARDS?

**When I avoid writing, I might be getting:** (check all that apply)

- ☐ A temporary sense of control over my time.
- ☐ Protection from feeling boxed in by structure or expectations.
- ☐ Freedom from criticism, edits, or compromise.
- ☐ A break from pressure to produce or perform.
- ☐ The satisfaction of ignoring a task someone else wants me to do.
- ☐ The illusion that I'm still in charge (even if I'm not progressing).
- ☐ A way to hold on to creative "purity" instead of dealing with messier stages like revision.

Other hidden payoffs I've noticed:

_____

_____

_____

_____

 **JOURNAL PROMPT**
What do these hidden rewards cost you over time creatively, emotionally, or in your writing career?

# future payoffs

Now imagine that in the coming weeks and months, you stop fighting expectations and start writing on your own terms. You shift from resisting pressure to reclaiming your creative power. What might you gain from that approach? (Check all that apply.)

**If I move forward in my own way, I could gain:**

☐ Confidence that I can finish things without being forced.
☐ A stronger sense of authorship over my work and process.
☐ Creative habits that work with my values, not against them.
☐ More progress on projects I care about.
☐ Freedom from the tug-of-war between resistance and guilt.
☐ A clearer sense of my voice, style, and creative identity.
☐ A finished body of work that's fully mine.

## OTHER BENEFITS I WANT TO CLAIM

_____     _____

_____     _____

## DESIGN YOUR "WHY-I-CHOOSE-TO-WRITE" CARD

Sometimes, writing can start to feel like a demand, even though it's something you love. When that happens, resistance kicks in. But deep down, you're here because something inside you *wants* to write. In the space below, design your own "Why-I-Choose-to-Write" card. Use phrases, bullet points, colors, or even rebellious doodles. Make it feel like yours, and then place it somewhere you can see it daily.

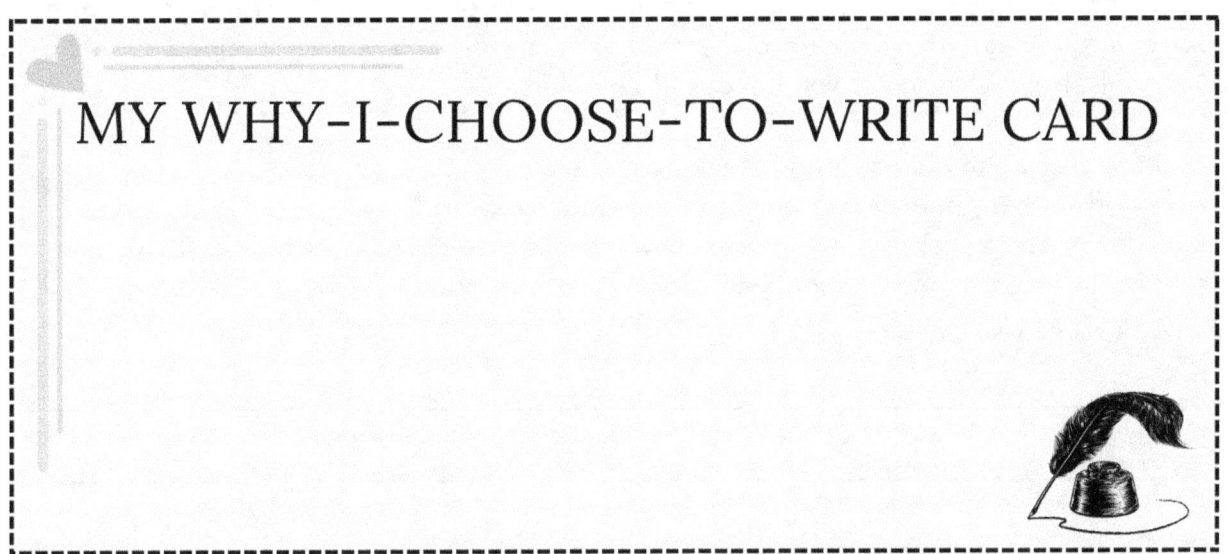

MY WHY-I-CHOOSE-TO-WRITE CARD

# your new writer identity

**Your way forward is yours to claim.**

When you see yourself as "someone who always resists," you reinforce that identity every time you delay a project, rebel against structure, or abandon something that starts to feel like a demand. Overcoming procrastination requires a shift in identity. You get to be the writer who chooses how to show up. You find ways to feel more ownership over your tasks. When you move from "I do what I want" to "I do what I choose, consistently," you become more powerful, not less.

## MY WRITING IDENTITY SHIFT

### Step 1: How do you see yourself now?

Let's get honest: What messages do you carry about yourself as a writer? Here are some common Defier identity thoughts:

- "I can't stick to a routine. It just doesn't work for me."
- "Deadlines kill my creativity."
- "The more I have to write, the less I want to."
- "I always rebel when someone tries to tell me how to do it."

Now, write 3 beliefs, labels, or self-messages you often carry about yourself as a writer.

_____

_____

_____

### Step 2: Who do you want to become?

Now imagine yourself six months from now. You've been showing up regularly and making your own choices. You've found a rhythm that fits you, and you've stopped resisting your own goals. Now what might you believe? Examples:

- "I set my own standards and I meet them."
- "I work with my energy and instincts, not against them."
- "I don't need to rebel to stay free. My voice is my freedom."
- "I make creative commitments and follow through because I want to."

Write 3 beliefs you want to grow into.

_____

_____

_____

**Step 3: What would that version of you do next?**
Next, using the ideas you wrote down, create a simple statement that captures who you are becoming as a writer.

Try this formula:
**Even though I usually _____, I'm learning to _____.**

Here are some examples:
- "Even though I usually reject structure, I'm learning to shape my own systems and stick to them."
- "Even though I usually lose interest when something becomes a 'should,' I'm learning to keep going for me."
- "Even though I usually resist expectations, I'm learning to follow through on what I care about."

## MY IDENTITY BRIDGE STATEMENT

_____

_____

_____

## ENCOURAGE YOURSELF!

**Remember:** Every time you choose to create even if you're feeling a little bit controlled by outside forces, you're shaping the writer you're becoming. You don't need to fight everything to stay free. Your freedom is already built into your voice, your vision, and your power to follow through.

> # Rather than resisting, I'm finding freedom in owning my own work.

# tools to write on your terms

**Structure doesn't have to mean control, especially when you create it.**

You thrive on creative freedom. But sometimes, your need to resist anything that feels like pressure can block you from finishing the work you care about most. That's why you need tools that respect your independence and keep you moving.

Think of these as creative tricks—not rules! You don't need to use all of them. Just pick the ones that help you feel more in charge of your writing life without getting stuck in cycles of rebellion and avoidance.

## TOOLKIT FOR THE DEFIER

### Use the "Because I Said So" Rule

When you catch yourself resisting, pause and reframe. Say: "I'm doing this because I choose to. No one else is the boss of my writing."

### Set Rebel-Friendly Goals

Set creative goals that don't feel rigid. For example: "Write for 10 minutes," "Draft the part I'm most excited about," or "Break a writing rule on purpose today."

### Design a Flexible Writing Menu

Instead of a to-do list, create a menu of options. That way you can choose what to do based on your mood and energy, while still making progress.

### Rebel with Purpose

If you're resisting a task (like revising or outlining), ask: "What's the real reason I don't want to do this?" Then write a different way that still gets you closer to your goal.

### Play the "I Dare You" Game

Challenge yourself to do one small thing, just to prove you can. For example: "I dare you to open your document and write a single snarky line."

### Ignore One Rule Today

Give yourself permission to break a "should"—write out of order, use passive voice, or skip the outline. It's your process. You get to decide.

### Claim Your Writing Space

Make your writing time feel like yours. Use a ritual, sound, or object that reminds you: This space belongs to me.

### Your Turn!

## CHOOSE TWO TOOLS

After reviewing the toolkit, pick two strategies that feel most helpful for you right now. For each one, write a small, clear action step you'll take to practice it this week.

*Examples:*
- If you choose the **Rebel-Friendly Goals** tool, your action step might be: "Pick one part of your project that excites you, and write for 10 minutes tomorrow."
- If you choose the **Writing Menu** tool, your action step could be: "Make a list of 3 writing tasks you can choose from this week."
- If you choose the **I Dare You** tool, your action step might be: "Open your draft and write one unexpected or defiant line today, just for the thrill of it."

## MY TOOLS AND ACTION STEPS

Tool #1 I'm Choosing:

_____

Action Step I'll Take:

_____

Tool #2 I'm Choosing:

_____

Action Step I'll Take:

_____

## THE DEFIER'S CREATIVE-POWER PHRASE

You need a sentence that reminds you why this is yours. Make it something that says: "I get to write this. I get to shape it. This is mine." This is your Creative Power Phrase. It states clearly that you're not following orders, but following your vision. Examples:

- "I write this my way, or not at all."
- "No one gets to decide how this story goes, not even my doubt!"
- "I'm not here to obey. I'm here to create."

**My creative-power phrase:**

_____

# mapping your novel journey

**Some writers need a map. Others carve paths no one's dared to follow.**

Rigid schedules can feel suffocating when you're a Defier. But if you wait for the right mood to strike, important projects may never get finished. The key is to choose your steps intentionally, so they still feel free, not pressured. This week, commit to three small actions. Each one should feel like something you choose.

## QUICK IDEAS FOR SMALL STEPS

(Choose or modify!)

- Write one defiant line just to get started.
- Create a "writing menu" of 3 tasks and pick whichever feels best.
- Revise one scene in a totally different style for fun.
- Set a 10-minute timer and write about anything—no rules allowed.
- Record a voice note ranting about your main character's flaws.
- List the genre rules you plan purposefully to ignore or bend.
- Cross out one writing rule you're sick of and do the opposite.

## MY SMALL STEPS FOR THE WEEK

| Day | One small action... | Did I take it? |
|---|---|---|
| Monday | | |
| Tuesday | | |
| Wednesday | | |
| Thursday | | |
| Friday | | |
| Saturday | | |
| Sunday | | |

## NOVEL-WRITING ROADMAP

### Step 1: Find your way in.

- Let your writing session be short, strange, or wildly out of order.
- Freewrite a dramatic moment, bold line of dialogue, or character confrontation.
- Ask yourself: "What would feel fun, fierce, or forbidden to write today?"

*Examples:*
- "I want to explore how my protagonist snaps under pressure."
- "I'm not ready for plot, so I'll write a letter between two characters instead."

**My stepping-in option:**

_____

### Step 2: Shape a loose structure.

- Jot a one-sentence summary of your novel's heartbeat (not the plot—the passion).
- Choose 3-5 turning points or emotional beats that matter to you.
- Create a visual, scene collage, playlist, or voice note brainstorm.

*Examples:*
- Key beats: Realization ➤ Confrontation ➤ Escape ➤ Betrayal ➤ New truth
- Loose structure: "Opening in winter - Something breaks - She runs - He follows"

**My loose structure:**

_____

### Step 3: Create your own writing routine.

- End each writing session with a creative dare. Leave yourself a challenge like: "Write the part no one expects," or "What rule can I break next?"
- Start with a permission ritual. Before you begin, remind yourself: "This is mine. I don't owe this to anyone."

*Examples:*
- Write a one-line defiance mantra on the page: "This belongs to no one but me."
- "What would I write if no one else were watching?"

**My own writing routine:**

_____

# carry your authority forward

**Real power comes from choosing what matters and seeing it through.**

When you use your voice to build, not just to resist, you become more than a rebel. You become an author in the truest sense: someone who designs their own creative life. The thoughts below show how Defier resistance can evolve into creative authority. Use them to reframe your thinking and reconnect with the part of you that wants to finish, on your own terms.

## SHIFT YOUR SELF-TALK

| Defiant Thought | Authority Reframe |
|---|---|
| "I'm not doing what they told me to." | "I'm doing this because I chose it." |
| "Deadlines make me shut down." | "I set timelines that match my rhythm." |
| "I don't want to write today." | "I can still take one step and stay in charge of my path." |
| "Routines ruin my creativity." | "I create rituals that protect my freedom and flow." |

**Your Turn**

Write down a Defiant thought and answer with a new authority-focused voice.

| Defiant Thought | Authority Reframe |
|---|---|
|  |  |
|  |  |
|  |  |
|  |  |

## YOUR PRO-AUTHORITY PLAN

**1. What's one way I can remind myself I'm choosing this path—no one else?**
(Example: Changing my desktop background to say "I decide why.")

_____

**2. What's a creative boundary or rule I want to rewrite this month?**
(Example: Revise in the middle of drafting if it helps me stay connected.)

_____

**3. What does writing on my terms look like in action?**
(Example: Choosing which project to write based on what excites me today.)

_____

## LOOKING BACK

Every time you shift from resistance to creative authority, you're proving to yourself that freedom and follow-through can coexist. You can direct your inner rebel toward what you care about. The old habits of pushback, defiance, and the instinct to delay may still show up. But you have something new now:

- Awareness of how resistance shows up in your writing life.
- Tools that protect your independence and support your progress.
- A clearer creative identity grounded in self-leadership.
- Evidence that you can move forward without giving up what makes you _you._

# authority commitment

*I commit to leading my writing life in a way that's bold, self-directed, and entirely mine.*

Signed: _____

Date: _____

# putting it together

# navigating the blend

**For Writers Who Identify With More Than One Type**

If your quiz results showed that you're affected by more than one type, this chapter is for you. Many writers have a blend of two, three, or even four procrastination patterns. Maybe you're a Dreamer-Perfectionist who also feels drained like the Tired type. Or a Fun-Seeker who becomes a Crisis-Maker under pressure.

Understanding your blend gives you power. It helps you recognize not just what's tripping you up, but how those traps interact. In this section, we'll help you name your blend more clearly, uncover how your patterns may reinforce one another, and develop a personalized response to those tangled tendencies.

## ACTIVITY 1: DEFINE YOUR TYPE BLEND

Each of your top types is likely to show up in your writing life in different ways. Sometimes it will be clear what's going on, but other times, not so much. Before we explore how they blend together, take a moment to list the types that resonated with you most, and reflect briefly on how each one tends to affect your writing behavior.

Here are a few examples to get you thinking:
- **The Worrier:** I often hesitate to begin because I'm afraid I'll mess it up or won't do the idea justice.
- **The Dreamer:** I love brainstorming and imagining, but I avoid the work of actually developing or revising.
- **The Overdoer:** I take on too much, so by the time I sit down to write, I have no creative energy left.

Now it's your turn. Use the table below to list up to 6 types you most strongly relate to, along with a short note about how each one shows up in your writing life.

| TYPE | HOW IT SHOWS UP |
|---|---|
|  |  |
|  |  |
|  |  |
|  |  |
|  |  |
|  |  |

## HOW DO THESE PATTERNS INTERACT?

Now that you've named your types individually, let's explore how they mix together.

Many writers experience their procrastination not in isolated moments, but in cycles, where one pattern feeds another. Maybe your inner Perfectionist slows you down, so you avoid the task, and then your Guilt type kicks in. Or maybe your Distracted type leads you into idea-hopping, which triggers your Disorganized type, and soon you're buried under chaos.

Here's a simple formula you can use to explore how your patterns interact:

**"When I feel _____ (type/emotion), I usually _____ (behavior), which then leads to _____ (new emotion or reaction)."**

You can also use:

**"My _____ type shows up first, which triggers my _____ type, and I often end up _____."**

Here are a few examples:

- "My Perfectionist slows me down, which frustrates my Distracted type, so I start scrolling instead of revising."
- "I feel too tired to write (Tired), so I overcompensate by doing something productive that's not writing (Avoider)."
- "I'm excited by new ideas (Dreamer), but as soon as I hit a hard part, I panic (Worrier) and switch to something else."

**Take a moment now to describe how your blend tends to show up in real time. What's the chain reaction you've noticed? What's the common loop?**

Use this space to write freely.

## ACTIVITY 2: SPOT THE PATTERN LOOPS

Think of your procrastination cycle like a row of dominoes. One gets bumped, and the rest start to fall. But something has to set it off. It might be a feeling, like anxiety, pressure, boredom, or tiredness. Or it might be a trigger moment, like opening your draft or getting a critique.

### Step 1: Identify Your First Domino

Ask yourself:
- What happens right before I shut down, check out, or avoid my writing?
- What feeling or situation seems to predict that I'll get stuck?
- What kinds of thoughts or triggers show up at the very beginning of a bad writing day?

Here are a few general first domino examples:
- You open your manuscript and feel overwhelmed before writing a single word.
- You get a spark of excitement about a new idea, but instantly feel pressure to do it "right."
- You sit down to write but realize you're exhausted and reach for your phone instead.

Here are some common first dominos by type:

| TYPE | HOW IT SHOWS UP |
|---|---|
| **Worrier** | Imagining everything that could go wrong before you start. |
| **Avoider** | Feeling uncomfortable, so you find something "productive" to do. |
| **Dreamer** | Excited by ideas, but avoiding structure to develop them. |
| **Fun-Seeker** | Feeling bored by your current writing task. |
| **Perfectionist** | Feeling the pressure to get it perfect from the very first sentence. |
| **Crisis-Maker** | Having plenty of time, but no urgency to begin. |
| **Distracted** | Sitting down to write, then thinking of five other things. |
| **Overdoer** | Being too booked or stretched thin to create real writing time. |
| **Guilty** | Thinking about how long it's been since you last wrote. |
| **Disorganized** | Sitting down to write but not being able to find what you need. |
| **Overthinker** | Getting stuck on one decision and spinning out. |
| **Tired** | Feeling mentally or physically drained before you even begin. |
| **Defier** | Feeling like you should write, yet rebelling against it. |

Use these examples as a springboard. What's your first domino? What gets bumped before everything else falls? Write it here:

_____

## Step 2: Write Your Domino Chain

Once you've spotted your first domino, the rest usually follow in sequence. One emotion triggers another. One avoidance leads to another excuse. Before you know it, an entire writing session has slipped away. These domino chains have a logic of their own. If you can see the pattern, you can begin to interrupt it.

*Example 1:*
I open my document and panic I'm not going to write well today (Worrier).
→ I can't find the scene I was looking for (Disorganized).
→ So I organize my office instead of writing (Disorganized/Avoider).

*Example 2:*
I'm excited about a new idea (Dreamer).
→ But I immediately feel pressure to get it right (Perfectionist).
→ I decide to "do more research" instead of writing anything (Overthinker).

*Example 3:*
I plan to write after work but I'm wiped out (Tired).
→ I scroll on my phone to recover. (Distracted)
→ Then I feel guilty (Guilty) and promise to write tomorrow, but don't.

Now it's your turn to explore what usually happens after your first domino gets pushed.

**1. My first domino (trigger, thought, or feeling—the one you wrote above):**

_____

**2. What that triggers (the next reaction or behavior):**

_____

**3. What I usually do next:**

_____

**4. How I feel after that:**

_____

**5. What I say to myself in that moment:**

_____

### Step 3: Sketch Your Cycle

Let's try another angle: Sketching your pattern! This can help you spot your cycle faster next time. Don't worry—you don't have to draw well. This is just to help externalize your process so you're not stuck replaying it in your head. Here are some tips:

### Option 1: Use arrows
Write each step of your pattern and connect them with arrows.
*Example:* Excited to Write → Feel Pressure → Overthink → Avoid → Feel Guilty

### Option 2: Use dominoes
Draw a row of rectangles like falling dominoes. Inside each one, write the emotion, thought, or behavior that happens in sequence.
*Example:* Worried → Stuck → Scroll phone → Feel guilty → Promise tomorrow

### Option 3: Draw a spiral
Start with your first feeling or thought in the center or at the top. Then spiral inward or downward as each step of your pattern follows. This works well if your procrastination tends to feel like it pulls you into a loop or downward slide.

### Option 4: Make a mini comic strip
If you're feeling playful, draw three small boxes side by side. In each one, sketch a stick figure version of what's happening.

### Bonus tip:
You can also use emojis, shapes, or symbols if drawing isn't your thing. A simple circle or square with a keyword in it—like "panic," "check email," or "scrolling"—can make the pattern visible without needing anything fancy.

There's no wrong way to do this. Just have fun with it and don't censor yourself. You're just trying to understand your writing patterns so you can change them.

### MY PROCRASTINATION CYCLE SKETCH:

 **PATTERN INTERRUPT TIP: CATCH IT EARLY**

Once you've identified your first domino, you can start changing the outcome by interrupting the chain as soon as it begins. You want to catch it from the very start if you can. This is called a pattern interrupt—a small, intentional shift that breaks your usual response and gives you a new option.

Here's how to use it:

1. **Notice the first domino** (panic, fatigue, distraction, etc.).
2. **Pause—take a breath or count to five.**
3. **Name it**—"This is my [Worrier] type showing up."
4. **Choose a small redirect**—a mindset reframe, a five-minute writing task, or a calming action that reconnects you to your goal.

You can even use this phrase as a reset: "This is the moment I usually get stuck. But today, I'm choosing something different."

Write it down. Stick it on your desk. Say it out loud when the pattern begins. Even the smallest interruption can change everything over time.

---

## ACTIVITY 3: IDENTIFY YOUR CROSSOVER CUES

When you have more than one dominant procrastination type, there are moments where the lines between them blur. These are called crossover cues—situations, tasks, or emotions that activate multiple patterns at once.

These can be especially tricky, because you're not just dealing with one stuck point, but navigating a cluster of habits, emotions, and avoidance strategies that are all firing at once.

Think of it like this: You're about to revise a scene. You feel tired (Tired type), afraid of doing it wrong (Worrier), and overwhelmed by all your open tabs (Disorganized). That single task triggered three types. And when those patterns pile up, it's much easier to walk away entirely.

In this next activity, you'll learn how to recognize those high-risk situations where your patterns converge so you can plan for them, respond with clarity, and avoid sliding into shutdown mode.

**Step 1: How to Spot a Crossover Cue**

Look for moments when:
- You feel multiple types of resistance at the same time.
- Your internal thoughts are contradictory or tangled ("I'm too tired to write, but also mad at myself for not doing it").
- You tend to abandon the task altogether and tell yourself you'll start fresh "tomorrow" (but often don't).

**Example 1: Editing a Draft**

- **Types Activated:** Perfectionist + Overthinker
- **Crossover Cue:** You try to revise one paragraph, but keep rewriting it over and over. You're never satisfied with the result, and you start overanalyzing every word choice and sentence structure until you feel mentally drained and stuck.
- **Why It Happens:** The Perfectionist in you is chasing an ideal version of the scene that may not exist, while the Overthinker is second-guessing every decision—what should stay, what should change, and what readers might think. Together, they paralyze your ability to move forward.

**Example 2: New Project Idea**

- **Types Activated:** Dreamer + Worrier + Defier
- **Crossover Cue:** You get an exciting idea for a new story and feel inspired until it's time to sit down and develop it. Suddenly, doubts creep in: What if I mess it up? What if I can't do this idea justice? Then, as soon as you try to outline or create a plan, you feel an inner resistance. You rebel against the structure and shut the notebook.
- **Why It Happens:** The Dreamer loves imagining new stories, but struggles with follow-through. The Worrier gets triggered by fear of failure or imperfection. Then the Defier kicks in when the process starts feeling restrictive or like "work," causing you to resist even your own creative plan.

**Example 3: Late Writing Session**

- **Types Activated:** Tired + Avoider + Guilty
- **Crossover Cue:** You planned to write in the evening, but when the time comes, you feel physically and mentally worn out. Instead of opening your document, you start tidying the house or checking emails—something that feels productive, but avoids the emotional risk of writing. Later, you lie in bed feeling bad about it.
- **Why It Happens:** The Tired type shows up when your energy is low, making writing feel impossible. The Avoider steps in to steer you toward safer tasks that don't require vulnerability or focus. Then the Guilty type quietly turns it all into self-blame, leaving you emotionally depleted and even less likely to write tomorrow.

## Step 2: Identify Your Own Crossovers

Now it's your turn to spot where your types tend to overlap. Start by thinking about writing situations where you consistently get stuck or where something feels harder than it should. These are often your "crossover zones."

Here are a few questions to help you find those moments:

*Is there a specific part of the writing process that always throws me off? (Starting? Finishing? Revising?)*

_____

*When do I find myself choosing something else instead of writing?*

_____

*Are there emotional patterns I've noticed, like dreading a writing session or talking myself out of it?*

_____

*Is there a "cue" or moment when I know I'm about to spiral?*

_____

Once you've identified a few of these sticky points, reflect on which types show up in each one. You can look back at the descriptions or your earlier work in this chapter to help you.

### Crossover Writing Situation #1:

What's happening:

_____

Types I think are being triggered:

_____

How those types seem to interact:

_____

**Crossover Writing Situation #2:**

What's happening:

_____

Types I think are being triggered:

_____

How those types seem to interact:

_____


**Crossover Writing Situation #3:**

What's happening:

_____

Types I think are being triggered:

_____

How those types seem to interact:

_____

# Build Your Blended Response Plan

Now that you've named your top types, tracked how they interact, and identified your crossover moments, it's time to put that insight to use. This is where you stop feeling caught off guard and start getting intentional.

A response plan is simply a way to prepare for the moments you know will come—when the web tightens, the old thoughts show up, and you're tempted to check out, shut down, or "do it later."

This section will help you create your plan, based on your patterns, your writing life, and your creative goals.

## Step 1: Spot Your Repeat Triggers

Looking back at your earlier exercises, what are the most common situations that cause your blended procrastination patterns to appear? Write down two or three that seem to happen often.

Trigger #1:

_____

Trigger #2:

_____

Trigger #3 (optional):

_____

## Step 2: Choose One Strategy for Each

Now match each of those triggers with a simple, low-pressure response. This might be a tool, a mindset shift, a calming action, or even a question you ask yourself. Think small. This is about interrupting the pattern, not solving everything in one move.

Here are a few examples to help you:
- When I feel tired before writing, I'll set a 5-minute timer and just start, even if I delete it later.
- When I want to avoid a hard scene, I'll move to a different scene or brainstorm instead of quitting entirely.
- When I panic about writing it "wrong," I'll remind myself that first drafts are allowed to be messy.

Now write your own below:

Response to Trigger #1:

_____

Response to Trigger #2:

_____

Response to Trigger #3 (optional):

_____

**Step 3: Write Your Go-To Reframe**
Choose one sentence or phrase you can say to yourself when things start to go sideways. Something that calms you, motivates you, or helps you remember the bigger picture.

Here are some examples:
- "This is the part where I usually shut down. But I don't have to follow that path today."
- "My patterns are real, but they're not the boss of me!"
- "I'm allowed to write badly. That's how I get to writing well."

**My Reframe:**

_____

_____

**Step 4: Keep It Visible**
This isn't just a one-time plan. It's something you can revisit, revise, and reuse every time the web starts to tighten.

You might want to:
- Post your reframe on your desk.
- Save your responses in a note on your phone.
- Re-copy them into a journal or planner each week.

Whatever you do, keep it close. Because this time, when the pattern shows up, you'll be ready.

# response plan tracker

Once you've created your response plan, the next step is to try it out in real life. This tracker gives you space to reflect on a moment when your pattern showed up and how you responded. Use it as often as you like. The more you observe without judgment, the more power you'll gain to choose something different next time.

**Date:** _____

**What was the writing situation?**
(Describe what was happening—time of day, what you were working on, etc.)

_____

_____

**What procrastination types showed up?**
(List any thoughts, behaviors, or feelings you recognized.)

_____

_____

**What was the "first domino"?**
(That initial trigger or cue that usually starts the spiral.)

_____

**What response or tool did you try?**
(From your blended plan—what small step, reframe, or strategy did you use?)

_____

**What happened after that?**
(What changed? How did you feel? Did it help, even a little?)

_____

_____

**Anything you'd like to try differently next time?**

_____

_____

# Keep Going

Procrastination doesn't vanish overnight. But now, you've done something most writers never do: You've looked beneath the surface. You've started to understand your patterns, labeling them to bring them into your awareness, then working with them compassionately and creatively. Keep this plan close. Come back to it when the web tightens again. And remember: progress doesn't have to be fast to be real.

> ## I recognize my patterns so I can choose my next move.

# CHAPTER 17

# when the web returns

## Troubleshooting Setbacks, Stalls, and Emotional Spirals

You were doing well. You were showing up. Maybe not every day, but more than before. You were thinking differently, writing more regularly, and feeling hopeful again. And then, something happened.

Maybe life got busy. Or your inner critic got loud. Maybe you just got tired. Now here you are, back in the familiar tangle of avoidance, self-blame, and frustration. The web has pulled you back in.

Falling off track is part of every growth cycle. Instead of seeing it as proof that you failed, see it as an opportunity to respond differently this time. This chapter will help you pause, reset, and reconnect with your path.

## ACTIVITY 1: FIND YOUR TRIGGERS

### Spot What's Really Happening

First, let's slow down and take an honest look at what pulled you off track. Falling back into procrastination can feel like it "just happened," but there's usually something underneath it. Noticing the moment before you slipped is one of the most powerful skills you can develop.

To help you out, here are a few common triggers that inspire procrastination:
- A busy week turned into a busy month.
- One missed writing session became a week of avoidance.
- An emotional crash or unexpected stressor stole your creative energy.
- Doubt or comparison crept in and shut you down.
- A moment of perceived "failure" made you question if you're cut out for this.

To find your trigger, here are a few questions to help you dig deep into your memory:
- What was happening in your life right before you stopped writing?
- Was there a task you were avoiding, or one that felt too big or unclear?
- Did you feel emotionally off? (Tired, discouraged, self-critical, disconnected?)
- Did something shake your confidence, like negative feedback or a lack of results?
- Were you trying to do too much, or pushing yourself too hard?

**The moment things slipped for me was:**

---

**I noticed myself avoiding or disconnecting when:**

_____

_____

Now try to dive deeper to see if you can name the emotional trigger behind the behavior.

For example:

- If you stopped writing for a few days and avoided opening your project, the behavior might be procrastination, but the emotional trigger could be fear ("What if this next part doesn't work?") or discouragement ("This is harder than I thought it would be").
- If you kept yourself busy with chores or other tasks, the behavior might look like productivity, but the emotional trigger could be self-doubt ("Who am I to write this?") or overwhelm ("There's too much going on—I can't think clearly.")

**What was really going on underneath?**

_____

_____

Sometimes just naming the feeling is the first step toward taking your power back.

## ACTIVITY 2: INTERRUPT THE SPIRAL

### Stop It Before It Goes Too Far

Falling off track isn't the problem. It's what we tell ourselves afterward that keeps us tangled in the web. You miss one session, then another. Soon you're not just avoiding your writing, but criticizing yourself for avoiding it. That inner spiral is what deepens the rut and makes it harder to climb out.

Here are some common spiral thoughts writers experience:

- "See? I'll never be consistent."
- "I always do this."
- "Why bother starting again if I'm just going to quit again?"

These thoughts feel convincing in the moment, but they are not facts. They are old mental grooves and you can write new ones.

**What do you usually say to yourself?**

_____

**What could you say instead?**
It's time to give yourself a compassionate, truthful, and empowering message that invites you back to writing.

Here's a simple formula to try:

**"Yes, I [acknowledge the truth of what happened], but I [affirm a gentle, forward-moving choice]."**

*Examples:*

- "Yes, I avoided writing this week, but I can still take one small step today."
- "Yes, I fell off track, but I've come back before and I can again."
- "Yes, I got stuck in my pattern, but I'm learning how to shift it, and that counts."

**My reset phrase:**

---

## ACTIVITY 3: RESET WITH SMALL WINS

### Make One Important Move
The best way to climb out of a creative slump is to make one small move that reminds your brain, "I can do this." You build momentum in moments. When you're tangled in a pattern, the most powerful thing you can do is start with something so small, it's almost impossible to fail.

### Gentle Reset Ideas

Here are some quick, light-touch resets that are deliberately low-pressure. Choose one that matches how you're feeling or that speaks to your dominant procrastination type. You can always make up one of your own.

### If you're a Worrier:
- Write one sentence and say out loud, "That was enough for today."
- Make a list of everything you already know about your next scene—no pressure to write it yet.
- Visualize your finished project and write down three reasons it matters.

### If you're Tired:
- Lie down and imagine your character's voice for five minutes. No writing required, but if you become inspired, by all means, go write!
- Set a timer for 3 minutes. Write one sentence. Then give yourself permission to stop.
- Read a page of something you love and let it lead you back to your story.

**If you're a Perfectionist:**
- Freewrite 100 words about anything you like, with a rule that you're not allowed to fix anything.
- Open your current project and highlight 5 things you like.
- Rename your draft "The Messy Version That Will Get Better."

**If you're a Dreamer:**
- Pick one idea from your list and sketch out what it might look like at the end.
- Set a 10-minute timer to write "about" your project—not the actual project.
- Choose a soundtrack and create a "scene vibe" for your next chapter.

**If you're Distracted:**
- Set a 5-minute timer to focus on one sentence only. Ignore the rest of the project.
- Turn off one digital distraction for 30 minutes and see how your brain feels.
- Keep a notebook nearby and jot down distracting thoughts as they pop up, then return to writing.

**If you're Disorganized:**
- Locate your current draft and label it clearly. Give it a fun new file name.
- Spend five minutes creating a mini "writing station" with only the tools you need.
- Choose one unfinished task (e.g., naming a character or outlining a chapter) and finish just that.

**If you're a Crisis-Maker:**
- Choose one writing task and pretend it's due in one hour. Set a timer and go.
- Schedule a "fake deadline" and ask a friend to check in.
- Write a short scene with intentionally high tension to create your own adrenaline.

**If you're a Fun-Seeker:**
- Write a scene that's purely entertaining, even if it doesn't fit your current project.
- Try dictating your writing instead of typing. Make it a game!
- Pair your writing session with a treat: favorite drink, music, or writing outdoors.

**If you're an Avoider:**
- Gently ask yourself what you're afraid of. Write just one honest sentence in response.
- Choose a writing task that feels emotionally neutral—something low-stakes.
- Create a "just show up" ritual: light a candle, open your doc, sit for 2 minutes.

**If you're Guilty:**
- Forgive yourself in writing. One paragraph, no edits.
- Write a short "I'm starting again" letter to yourself.
- Remind yourself how hard you've been trying. Make a list of ways you've shown up.

**If you're an Overthinker:**
- Set a 5-minute limit to make one decision you've been stuck on. Go with your gut.
- Write the worst possible version of the sentence or scene you've been overanalyzing—on purpose!
- Choose a task that doesn't require a decision, like copying out your favorite passage.

**If you're a Defier:**
- Change up your space or method. Write in a notebook instead of on your laptop.
- Choose your own writing prompt instead of one that feels assigned.
- Say aloud: "I don't have to write, but I'm going to anyway, because I decided to."

**If you're an Overdoer:**
- Do only one writing task today and celebrate that as a win.
- Cross off or postpone something else to create space for writing.
- Give yourself 15 guilt-free minutes to write without multitasking.

**Choose Your Reset**

Now it's your turn. Look over the list above and pick one, or create your own.

**One small reset I can try this week is:**

_____

**When I plan to do it:**

_____

## ACTIVITY 5: CREATE AN EMOTIONAL RESET RITUAL

**Sometimes You Need a Soft Restart**

Falling off track is often more emotional than logical. You don't just lose time, but momentum, confidence, and sometimes even your connection to yourself as a writer. That's why it helps to create a reset ritual—something small and symbolic that reminds you: you're still a writer, and you can start again at any time.

A reset ritual doesn't have to be fancy. It just needs to feel grounding. It's a way of saying, "I'm here. I'm ready to try again."

On the next page are some ideas tailored to your specific type. You can use them as-is, mix and match, or come up with your own.

| Type | Reset Ritual |
|---|---|
| **Worrier** | Light a candle and whisper, "It's okay to begin scared." Then open your draft and write one sentence without judging it. |
| **Avoider** | Hold your writing notebook or open your file. Say: "This isn't dangerous. It's just a page." Then freewrite anything. |
| **Dreamer** | Play music that matches the mood of your story. Let your imagination wander there before returning to the page. |
| **Fun-Seeker** | Put on your favorite upbeat song and dance it out for 30 seconds. Sit down smiling and write something fun. |
| **Perfectionist** | Close your eyes and repeat: "Done is better than perfect." Open your doc and type one intentionally messy line. |
| **Crisis-Maker** | Set a five-minute countdown and shout "Go!" out loud. Treat it like a timed challenge and make it fun. |
| **Distracted** | Put your phone in another room. Take three deep breaths with your eyes closed, then write the first word you think of. |
| **Overdoer** | Say no to one task that isn't urgent. Then sit with your writing—no multitasking, no guilt—for 10 quiet minutes. |
| **Guilty** | Write a short forgiveness note to yourself. "Dear me, it's okay to begin again." Then type a single sentence of your project. |
| **Disorganized** | Clear just one item from your writing space. Say aloud, "This is my space to create," and open your draft. |
| **Overthinker** | Flip a coin to decide your next writing step. Let the randomness free you. Then write for five minutes, no backspacing. |
| **Tired** | Wrap yourself in a blanket or put on cozy socks. Sip something warm and set a gentle timer for five quiet minutes of writing. |
| **Defier** | Change up your writing setting. Go outside, move to the floor, or use a notebook. Say, "I write on my own terms," and begin. |

**Your Ritual**

Now create a ritual of your own, or borrow one that speaks to you.

**My emotional reset ritual will be:**

_____

_____


## TIME TO CELEBRATE!

Let's celebrate your comeback. Pick one of these quick, fun actions to seal your reset and bring a little joy into the moment:

- Give yourself a dramatic fist pump and say, "I'm back, baby."
- Snap a picture of your writing space (messy or not!) and call it The Return Scene.
- Put a gold star, sticker, or goofy emoji next to today's planner entry.
- Text a writing friend: "Guess who just took the smallest possible step back into writing?"
- Open a blank page and type: This counts.
- Do one power pose. Bonus points for sound effects.
- Write a blog or series of social media posts about your comeback.
- Create an image in Canva or another program that symbolizes your comeback.

**Or create your own comeback move:**

_____

_____

 **JOURNAL PROMPT**

Journal about any other thoughts you have connected to comebacks.

# procrastination type chat

You've spent enough time wrestling with your procrastination, so let's flip the script. Instead of letting it spiral you, sit down and have a conversation. Get curious. Be playful. Ask it what it wants, and why it keeps showing up when you're trying to write. You might be surprised by what it says!

## YOUR MISSION

1. **Pick your dominant procrastination type** (or one that's currently showing up loudest).
2. **Imagine it as a character.** Give it a name, a voice, maybe even a dramatic flair. (The Overthinker might be a nervous academic in too-tight glasses. The Fun Seeker? A glitter-covered imp with a ukulele and no deadlines.)
3. **Start the dialogue.** Use the prompts below to get going, or make up your own lines.

*Example Starter:*

**YOU:** "We were supposed to write today. What happened?"
**TYPE:** "Oh, I meant to! But then I thought, shouldn't we clean the closet first? You need a creative environment!"
**YOU:** "Mmmhmm. And now it's 9 p.m."
**TYPE:** "But look how organized your sock drawer is!"
**YOU:** "Okay. Let's talk about what you're *really* afraid of."

### Try These Prompts—Ask Your Procrastination:

- "Why do you keep showing up right when I sit down to write?"
- "What are you trying to protect me from?"
- "How do you think you're helping me?"
- "What would it take for you to step aside, at least for now?"

**Bonus Twist:** Let your "Wise Writer Self" join the conversation at the end. What would they say to both of you? Let this be weird, imperfect, even funny. The goal is to remind yourself that you are not the pattern. You're the one listening, learning, and leading yourself forward.

_____    _____

_____    _____

_____    _____

_____    _____

_____    _____

CHAPTER 18

# freedom from the web 🕷

**Final Reflection, Celebration, and Empowering Next Steps**

Well here we are—near the end of the workbook! But hopefully, not the end of your transformation.

So far, you've stayed with this. You've looked at yourself with honesty, curiosity, and courage. You've untangled old thought patterns, faced uncomfortable emotions, and experimented with small, powerful steps toward change.

And you're wiser now. You know your patterns and what trips you up. More importantly, you know what helps you move through it.

Let this final chapter be your reminder that you don't need to wait for the perfect moment to write. You can begin again on any day, any page. Even right now.

Let's take a few final moments to honor the changes you've made and the ones that are still unfolding.

## LOOKING BACK TO MOVE FORWARD

Before we wrap up, let's pause to acknowledge what you've uncovered. This is a space to capture the key insights and shifts that have emerged during your journey.

**One thing I now understand about my procrastination is:**

_____

**One mindset that shifted for me during this process:**

_____

**One tool or practice I want to keep using:**

_____

**One message I want to carry forward as a writer:**

_____

# final reflection: claiming your freedom

Now that you've looked back, let's look forward with intention, clarity, and self-trust. Take this moment to define what freedom from the writer's web means to you. What might your future look like now? What possibilities are opening up for you? There are no right answers here, only your truth, your growth, and your next brave steps. Set the stage for an exciting writing future!

**One belief I'm choosing to let go of:**

_____

**One belief I want to carry forward:**

_____

**What freedom from the writer's web means to me:**

_____

_____

_____

```
MY FREEDOM DECLARATION

Complete this sentence with your own words, or use it as inspiration:

From this day forward, I choose to show up for my writing with

_____, even when _____.

Or try your own:

_____

Signature: _____ Date: _____
```

# a quiet celebration

Your wins may be small or even unnoticeable to other people. You might not be holding a finished novel, but maybe you wrote again, forgave yourself, or saw your patterns with new eyes. It's important to celebrate these little achievements, as it helps train your brain to keep it up! Not everyone celebrates the same way. Below are gentle celebration ideas inspired by your type. Try one that fits, or mix and match to make your own:

## CELEBRATIONS BY TYPE

| TYPE | HOW TO CELEBRATE |
|------|------------------|
| **Worrier** | Write a letter to your future self, celebrating the courage it took to keep showing up. |
| **Avoider** | Light a candle or touch your journal. Whisper, "I didn't avoid myself this time." |
| **Dreamer** | Create a vision board, playlist, or collage that represents your next writing chapter. |
| **Fun-Seeker** | Turn up your favorite song and dance it out—writing doesn't have to be serious! |
| **Perfectionist** | Post one line of messy writing, no matter how imperfect, somewhere visible. |
| **Crisis-Maker** | Spontaneous "victory dash"—go for a run, blast music, or set a new short-term challenge. |
| **Distracted** | Schedule 30 distraction-free minutes to do something you love. |
| **Overdoer** | Take something off your to-do list. Breathe. That empty space? That's your celebration. |
| **Guilty** | Say out loud, "I kept going. That matters." Then give yourself a small gift of some kind. |
| **Disorganized** | Organize a tiny corner of your writing space. Place a sticky note: Look how far I've come! |
| **Overthinker** | Write a silly haiku or nonsense line, just for fun. No thinking. Just write! |
| **Tired** | Take an intentional rest. Lie down, stretch, nap, or soak in a moment of quiet. |
| **Defier** | Celebrate on your terms. Break your usual routine and declare this moment yours. |

**My Celebration Ideas**

_____

_____

_____

# empowering next steps

In this next section, I'll help you choose a few simple, empowering steps you can carry with you. These steps are meant to support your freedom, creativity, and forward momentum as you go.

Think of these as **anchors.** When the web starts to tug again, these are the practices that will help you stay grounded, clear, and connected to your writing self.

## 1. MAINTAIN A SIMPLE WRITING RHYTHM

Create a gentle writing rhythm that feels doable and supportive.

- **Worrier:** Choose one safe, low-stakes task to start your sessions (like rereading yesterday's work).
- **Avoider:** Start sessions by writing about your resistance, then pivot to your project.
- **Dreamer:** Create a rotating schedule of writing tasks so you don't get bored. For example, planning one day, writing the next.
- **Fun-Seeker:** Gamify your rhythm—use stickers, rewards, setting changes, etc.
- **Perfectionist:** Commit to a "messy writing session" once a week—no editing allowed.
- **Crisis-Maker:** Set short, exciting sprints with pretend deadlines.
- **Distracted:** Use a simple timer (5-15 minutes) to create focused bursts with short breaks.
- **Overdoer:** Set a hard limit: one task per writing session. Stopping is the win.
- **Guilty:** Track your wins on a calendar or sticky note, and let every session, no matter how big or small, count.
- **Disorganized:** Choose one consistent writing spot and time of day to reduce decision fatigue.
- **Overthinker:** Limit your choices: just two writing tasks per session to reduce mental spiraling.
- **Tired:** Link your writing to a moment of rest (before coffee, after a walk, etc.) so it feels supported, not draining.
- **Defier:** Design your own rules. Make your writing rhythm feel rebellious and free.

**My Writing Rhythm Ideas**

_____

_____

_____

## 2. KEEP A RESET RITUAL NEARBY

Pick one reset ritual from the previous chapter and keep it visible somewhere—like on a sticky note, your phone, or in your planner. Use it any time the web starts to tighten again.

- Make it short.
- Make it easy to remember.
- Make it feel like an act of self-trust.

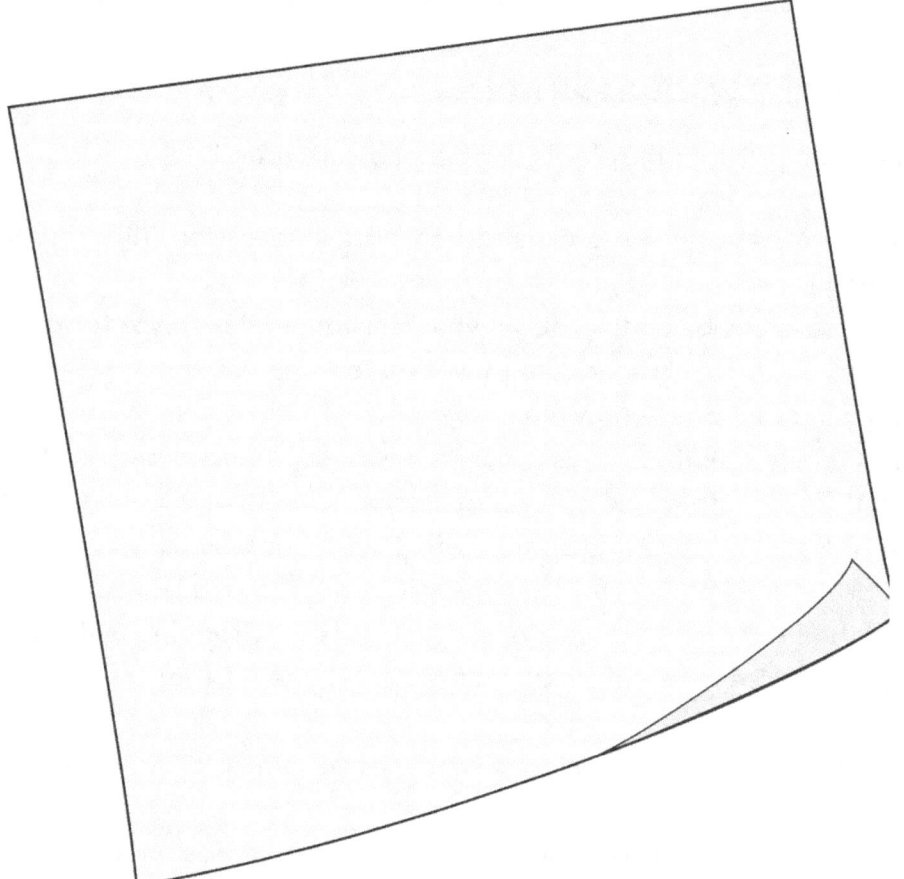

## 3. DECIDE THAT TODAY MATTERS

You don't need to plan a year ahead. You don't even need to know what next week looks like. Just decide: Today, I'm showing up. Even if it's for 3 minutes. Even if it's to write one sentence.

**What's one small thing I can do today to honor my writing life?**

_____

_____

# final words

If you're still holding this book, I want you to know that I'm proud of you! You didn't have to keep going. You could've stopped anywhere along the way, but you stayed with it. And that tells me something important: You care about your writing.

You might still feel unsure. That's okay. You don't have to feel confident every day. But I hope you believe this: You've changed. You've gotten to know yourself better. You've peeled back the noise and started to understand the real reasons you haven't been writing the way you want to. That's how freedom begins.

So if the web pulls at you again (which it probably will), don't give up. All you need to do is what you've done here: Gently lead yourself back one step at a time.

I'll be here, quietly cheering you on from my side of the page.  —*Colleen*

---

**MY WRITER'S FREEDOM MANIFESTO**

**I am a writer who...**

_____

**I no longer believe...**

_____

**I choose to...**

_____

**Even when the web returns, I will...**

_____

**My writing is worth it because...**

_____

**The story I'm telling myself is...**

_____

**Signature:** _____ **Date:** _____

# stay connected!

If this workbook helped you untangle your procrastination patterns, take braver steps toward your writing goals, or simply feel more seen in your creative life, I'd be so grateful if you'd leave a quick review on Amazon, Goodreads, or wherever you purchased the book. It would help spread the word to other writers!

And if you haven't picked up the main book yet, now's the perfect time. *Escape the Writer's Web* is the full guide that unpacks the emotional roots of writer procrastination and walks you through the *why* behind the patterns you've been exploring here. It's filled with insight, storytelling, and support to help you understand your type more fully, and start untangling the habits that have kept you stuck for far too long. This workbook is your action guide. The main book is your deeper understanding. Together, they make a powerful team.

If you'd like more writing encouragement, free resources, or updates on new tools and books as they're released, I'd love to stay in touch.
You can join my newsletter at:

www.masterwritermindset.com/newsletter

Find more of my nonfiction books for writers listed at the end of this book.
(Turn another page!)

Curious about my fiction? I also write historical fantasy and supernatural thrillers. If you'd like to explore those worlds, you can find free samples and more at:

www.colleenmstory.com

Whether this is the end of our journey or just a pause in it, thank you for being here. Keep writing. Keep discovering. And above all, keep showing up!

—*Colleen*

**Twitter:** @colleen_m_story  |  **Instagram:** @colleenmstory
**YouTube**: @ColleenMStoryteller  |  **LinkedIn:** Colleen M. Story

# acknowledgments

First and foremost, thank you to my family for your steady support of my writing life. Gerald and Mary, I'm especially grateful for your encouragement along the way.

To my wonderful newsletter subscribers—you inspire me to keep creating resources like this. I hope this workbook helped you untangle a few of the webs that have kept you from your words.

And to every writer who's ever struggled with procrastination: thank you for showing up. The world needs your voice, and I'm honored to support you in finding your way back to it.

# about the Author

**Colleen M. Story** writes award-winning historical fantasy, supernatural thrillers, and motivational books for writers. She grew up on a Colorado ranch making up stories on horseback, which probably explains a lot. A lifelong musician, she still plays French horn in the local symphony and teaches music on the side. With 25+ years as a freelance health writer, she's the unofficial "medical hotline" for friends and family. When she's not typing away, you'll probably find her at the movies—sci-fi, fantasy, action, or anything with a good chase scene. Find her books at colleenmstory.com or masterwritermindset.com.

# consider these other titles
# by colleen m. story

......................................................................................................

**OVERWHELMED WRITER RESCUE:** Stop drowning in your to-do list and start living a more joyful creative life! "If you read only one self help book this year – grab this one! It is not just for writers. This book is very motivating and so easy to read quickly." ~Laura's Reading

**WRITER GET NOTICED!:** Stop feeling invisible and start attracting the attention you deserve! "A Five Star must have in your library as an invaluable guide for writers. I found her information and self-discovery processes applicable in other aspects of my life as well!" ~Susan Violante, Reader Views

**YOUR WRITING MATTERS:** You start to wonder if you're wasting your time. Does your writing even matter? "I wish I'd been able to read this book when I was a beginning writer. . . . It would have helped me vanquish my self-doubts, ignore naysayers, and encouraged me to develop the craft of writing."
~Joe Wisinski for Readers' Favorite

**THE CURSE OF KING MIDAS:** This captivating tale of King Midas begins the new mythological fantasy series. "A gripping fantasy that blends classic myth with contemporary storytelling finesse . . . a standout in the genre."
~Foram Vyas for Readers' Favorite Book Awards

**THE GIMIRRI INVASION:** The gripping saga that began in The Curse of King Midas continues: "A vivid, engrossing tale . . . thoroughly absorbing, unpredictable, and powered by strong forces that both enlighten and create an incredible page-turner."
~D. Donovan, Sr. Reviewer, Midwest Book Review

**THE BEACHED ONES:** He came back, determined to keep his promise . . . "A poignant tale of forgiveness and redemption that reaches beyond the grave . . . will have you staying up late to accompany Daniel on his journey to the end."
~Melissa Payne, bestselling author of *The Secrets of Lost Stones*

**LOREENA'S GIFT:** A blind girl's terrifying "gift" allows her to regain her eyesight —but only as she ferries the recently deceased into the afterlife. "This book sucked me in and I couldn't turn the pages fast enough." ~JBronderBookReviews

www.ingramcontent.com/pod-product-compliance
Lightning Source LLC
Chambersburg PA
CBHW080804120626
46556CB00009B/3220